CW00433421

Dummies Guide to Starting Your Own Business

The Simplest, Step-by-Step Guide to Launch a Successful Small Business in Record Time – Begin Your Entreprenaurial Path Now

FINANCE KNIGHTS
PUBLICATIONS

TABLE OF CONTENT

Introduction

*A*re you sick of all these blogs and webinars that ask for your informations and require you to jump through hoops, promising vague value in return? Well, we're not hiding behind any of that. As a result, we have no intention of wasting your time with fluff during this entire book. Every single thing we share will be valuable, with no exceptions.

If you're here looking for overnight hacks, quick wins, or get-rich-quick schemes, this isn't the right place for you. This book is exclusively for dedicated business starters who are committed to sustainable, long-term growth. We're here to help you achieve the business and lifestyle you desire.

The information contained in this book, mirror what business coaches typically offer at premium prices, often costing thousands of dollars. I'm not suggesting that you shouldn't consider hiring a business coach if you believe it's beneficial; they can certainly provide tailored advice through personalized one-on-one sessions. However, the fundamental principles you'll find here align closely with their teachings.

Our goal is not to present you with some magical two or three-step process because, let's be honest, there's no one-size-fits-all solution in business. Every business and business owner is unique. Instead, we'll provide you with the right CEO mindsets, strategies, and frameworks, step by step. By this end, we hope you'll have a fresh perspective on your business and how to operate it.

Unfortunately, the truth is that most businesses fail, and even among the successful ones, very few make it to seven figures or beyond—maybe around three percent. That means 97 percent of businesses are going about it the wrong way. We want to uncover what most people do wrong and avoid those pitfalls. We'll learn from expensive mistakes, including my own, to save you years of struggle, costs, and frustration.

Some stuff might seem obvious, some can get a bit technical and dull, but trust me, once you soak it all in and finish this book, you'll be a different person, ready to roll and change your life.

I'll share proven frameworks that work, and we'll go through some case studies to illustrate the before-and-after transformation. If all of this aligns with your goals, grab your favorite beverage, get your notepad, pen, or tablet, and let's dive into this masterclass. By the end of it, you'll hopefully have a clear roadmap to take your business to the seven-figure and beyond level. Ready? Let's get started!

Chapter 1: The Entrepreneurial Journey

$\mathcal{W}$elcome to "Dummies Guide to Starting Your Own Business",

my name is Carmel (In the picture I am the human, the other is Ron) I'm the founder of Finance Knights Publications I'm going to

walk you through this first part of the book before I leave you to paragraphs that contain more technical notices. I want to share my insights on how to start a business step by step, covering the entire journey from preparation to registration and post-launch steps. I understand the challenges because when I embarked on my entrepreneurial journey in 2017, I was utterly clueless. I desired to work for myself, but I lacked any experience in entrepreneurship. Like many aspiring entrepreneurs, I devoured blogs, followed influencers, and immersed myself in motivational content.

I learned valuable lessons, but I remained overwhelmed and stuck in the same place. It was then that I decided to take charge, learn how to start a business from scratch, and discover what it truly entailed.

The fear of failure

Before diving into the tips, strategies, and steps, we must address something crucial starting. The fear of failure often paralyzes individuals who spend excessive time researching, planning, and budgeting without taking any meaningful action. I was once caught in this cycle, driven by a deep-seated fear of failure. To break free, try this exercise with me... no really, try it:

• Close your eyes and take a few deep breaths to relax.

• Imagine yourself standing at the base of a massive, majestic mountain.

• In your mind's eye, look up at the peak of the mountain, which rises higher than the clouds, up there, you find your goal, whatever it is.

• Feel the awe and inspiration that the mountain evokes. Let this motivate you to start your climb.

• Recognize that the fear of failure and the fear of starting are your biggest obstacles.

• Take a physical step forward, and say aloud, "I am starting my climb."

• Continue to move forward, one step at a time, as you progress, keep your focus on the next two meters in front of you.

• After a few minutes of "climbing," pause.

• Look back, and see how far you have come, become aware that you can do it, you only have to do one thing: ACTION. Step by step, you will get above the clouds.

Whenever you feel the urge to conduct more research, watch another video, or read another blog, pause and perform this exercise. Then, take your next tangible action step. This is the first key to overcoming the fear of failure and starting your business journey.

The case study: the story of Anthony, the plumber

Once upon a time in a bustling town named Brooksville, there lived a young and passionate hydraulic named Anthony. At the age of 26, he had already developed an exceptional skill set in the art of plumbing and hydraulics. Anthony loved his work more than anything else in the world. He had an uncanny ability to fix even the most complex plumbing problems, earning him a reputation as one of the finest plumbers in town.

However, there was one thing that always cast a dark cloud over Anthony's otherwise bright career – his loathsome chief, Mr. Reynolds. Mr. Reynolds was known for his dictatorial management style, his tendency to take credit for his employees' hard work, and his overall lack of appreciation for the talent and dedication of his team members.

For years, Anthony endured the daily grind of working under Mr. Reynolds' oppressive rule. He watched as his ideas were dismissed, his hard work went unrecognized, and his fellow plumbers grew increasingly demoralized. Anthony's passion for plumbing was slowly being overshadowed by his frustration with his chief.

One fateful day, after a particularly humiliating incident at work, Anthony made a life-changing decision. He decided that he had had enough of Mr. Reynolds and his toxic leadership. With unwavering determination, he quit his job and decided to pursue his passion on his terms.

Despite being a skilled hydraulic engineer, Anthony faced a significant challenge when it came to managing his plumbing business and attracting new customers. He recognized that his technical expertise alone wouldn't suffice to make his venture truly successful. Determined to bridge this gap, he decided to take matters into his own hands.

One day, he stumbled upon a realization: to thrive in the competitive world of plumbing, he needed to learn the art of marketing and entrepreneurship. Anthony embarked on a self-education journey that would change the trajectory of his business.

He delved into books on marketing strategies, customer acquisition, and successful entrepreneurship. Late into the night, he pored over pages filled with insights from renowned business leaders and marketing experts. His dedication to learning matched his passion for plumbing.

As he absorbed the wisdom from these books, Anthony began to understand how to offer higher-quality services and effectively reach a wider clientele. He implemented new marketing techniques, such as targeted advertising and online presence optimization, to showcase his expertise to potential customers.

After mastering marketing and reaching a wider clientele, Anthony realized that his skills and ambition could support a more significant endeavor. He decided to take the leap and open his own shop, offering a wide range of plumbing services, thermo plumbing items, home installations, and repairs. This move allowed him to provide a more comprehensive solution to his customers' needs.

As his shop gained popularity and the demand for his services continued to grow, Anthony recognized the need to expand his team. He sought out talented plumbers and professionals who shared his dedication to excellence. Anthony's vision was not only to provide top-notch plumbing solutions but also to build a team that could uphold his commitment to quality and customer satisfaction.

Over time, his team of skilled employees became an integral part of his business. They brought their expertise and passion for plumbing, contributing to the shop's success. Together, they expanded the scope of services they could offer, taking on more significant projects and serving a broader client base.

As the years passed, Anthony's business flourished. Anthony's reputation as a fair and compassionate boss grew as he treated his employees with respect, encouraged their ideas, and recognized their hard work. He created a work environment where everyone felt valued and appreciated.

Not content with just running successful plumbing shops, Anthony's entrepreneurial spirit led him to establish his own plumbing company. This company took on larger projects, from commercial buildings to municipal contracts, and soon became a household name in Brooksville.

In a surprising turn of events, Anthony found himself presented with an unexpected opportunity. Mr. Reynolds, the person whose management style had once frustrated Anthony, was facing dire circumstances with his struggling plumbing business. The shop was on the brink of bankruptcy, and Mr. Reynolds had no choice but to seek a way out.

Despite the history of their contentious relationship, Anthony saw this as a chance for transformation rather than vengeance. He recognized that his skills and entrepreneurial spirit could breathe new life into Mr. Reynolds' failing business. After negotiations and careful consideration, Anthony acquired Mr. Reynolds' shop.

In an ironic twist of fate, Mr. Reynolds, who had once been the chief in charge, now found himself in the unfamiliar position of an employee under Anthony's leadership. It was a situation neither of them had anticipated, and it was clear that Mr. Reynolds was less than thrilled about the arrangement.

Key Considerations of Anthony's Story

The distinctions between Anthony and Mr. Reynolds offer compelling insights into why Anthony ultimately found success. Let's pinpoint these crucial elements that set Anthony apart:

1. Continuous Learning: Anthony's thirst for knowledge and his dedication to self-education stood out prominently. He recognized that plumbing expertise alone wouldn't suffice in the evolving business landscape. His commitment to studying marketing and entrepreneurship allowed him to adapt and thrive.

2. Adaptability: Anthony's ability to adapt to changing circumstances and market demands was a defining characteristic. He embraced new ideas and approaches, while Mr. Reynolds clung to outdated methods. Anthony's adaptability allowed him to seize opportunities and navigate challenges effectively.

3. Customer-Centric Approach: Anthony understood the importance of putting the customer at the center of his business. He prioritized customer satisfaction, building trust and loyalty among his clientele. In contrast, Mr. Reynolds struggled to connect with and cater to customer needs effectively.

4. Entrepreneurial Vision: Anthony possessed a visionary mindset. He saw beyond the confines of his plumbing skills and envisioned a comprehensive service offering that included thermo-plumbing items, home installations, and repairs. This holistic approach expanded his business horizons.

5. Marketing Mastery: Anthony's transformation into a marketing-savvy entrepreneur set him apart. His ability to harness the power of a dedicated website, active social media presence, and targeted advertising significantly broadened his reach and customer base.

6. Leadership and Positive Workplace Culture: Anthony's leadership style, marked by mentorship and a commitment to fostering a positive workplace culture, played a pivotal role. His employees felt valued and motivated, contributing to the overall success of his business.

7. Resilience and Turning Challenges into Opportunities: Anthony's resilience in the face of adversity was evident throughout his journey. Instead of being deterred by challenges, he saw them as opportunities for growth and improvement.

This was Anthony's story, an inspired story that, however, retraced my father's path, I wanted to share it with you because it was for me an example of how a simple laborer with no special qualifications could create a successful business by simply never feeling like he has arrived and wanting to constantly keep improving himself. After many attempts, action after action, and mistake after mistake, he arrived at his goal without letting the difficulties in his life get him down.

The Entrepreneurial Journey

Transforming your passion into a lucrative endeavor requires more than just unwavering enthusiasm. You must pinpoint a crucial element that guarantees business success. As the saying goes, "Find something that feels like play to you but looks like work to others." This entails aligning your innate talents and interests (the passion) with something society values as work.

Josh Kaufman, in his insightful work, "The Personal MBA," suggests reflecting on basic human needs as a starting point. Humans often purchase products or services to satisfy five fundamental needs: feeling good about themselves, establishing connections, learning and growth, ensuring safety, and reducing effort. Identifying which of these needs your passion addresses is vital for practicality.

Promoting Your Unique Perspective

Being exceptionally skilled in your field means little if no one is aware of your expertise. Thus, the next step is honing your craft while generously sharing valuable information as proof of your skills. Whether through blog posts, tutorials, webinars, podcasts, or social media, providing free content serves a dual purpose. It allows you to improve your skills continually and builds trust with potential clients. Think of it as a free trial of your services.

To stand out amid a sea of competitors offering free content, leverage your unique perspective. Your distinct interpretation and presentation of information can provide fresh insights and resonate with your audience. Remember that the way you convey information can be just as crucial as the content itself.

Monetizing Your Passion with Confidence

Monetizing your passion can be challenging due to various psychological barriers, like fear of rejection, self-doubt, or discomfort about charging for your skills. However, it's essential to recognize that turning your passion into a business requires financial sustainability. By charging for your services or products, you're not just earning income; you're also enabling others to benefit from your expertise.

Moreover, be creative in exploring different revenue streams related to your passion. Don't limit yourself to a single income source. And remember, while financial success is crucial, focusing on the impact you make can help maintain the joy and motivation in your journey.

This book delves deeper into each step, offering comprehensive insights and practical advice.

Your passion has the potential to become a thriving business. Embrace the process, showcase your unique perspective, and confidently monetize your expertise. Your success story awaits.

Chapter 2: Finding Your Business Idea

Conceptualize

*I*t may seem like there are countless options for starting a business, but it's essential to approach this decision methodically. Start by considering the importance of beginning with a single, solid concept. To make the  right choice, you must evaluate specific factors that are relevant to you, such as your skills, experience, and passion for the business, industry, or target audience.

Ensure that the business idea you choose operates within a growing market or industry and has a high likelihood of success. For instance, let's take my experience as an example. When I launched my first business, it was a social media marketing agency. My partners and I were early adopters of platforms like Facebook, Twitter, and Instagram when they emerged a few years later. This gave us a significant advantage because we already possessed skills and experience in that domain.

Simultaneously, we had a strong passion for entrepreneurship and a desire to help others like us succeed in the business world. We recognized that, in 2011, companies were eager to explore how to harness social media for their benefit, indicating a substantial market potential. Additionally, although there weren't many social media marketing agencies at the time, the business model of a marketing firm was well-established and successful.

By examining these four critical factors—your skills, experience, passion, and market potential—you can tailor a business idea to suit your unique profile. Think about how you can combine your strengths with a proven business concept in a thriving market.

To begin, it's essential to recognize that there are three fundamental types of businesses you can start: service-based, product-based, and digital product-based. Service businesses provide various services to customers, ranging from lawn care and web design to hairstyling. Product businesses, on the other hand, focus on selling physical products—think Walmart, Amazon, or Etsy. Lastly, digital product businesses offer digital products or services, such as Netflix, Udemy, and online course creators.

Once you've grasped these options, the next step is to generate business ideas. You can kickstart this process by compiling three lists:

1. Types of Activities: Enumerate activities you genuinely enjoy, such as interacting with people, working independently, writing, filming, public speaking, or hands-on work. Consider whether you prefer an indoor or outdoor work environment.

2. Interests: Create a list of your personal interests or hobbies, which can span anything from gardening and chess to photography and animal care.

3. Skills: Note down any skills you possess, whether they come naturally to you or were acquired through training. These skills can encompass a wide array of competencies, such as patience, communication, writing, culinary arts, photography, or graphic design.

With these three lists in hand, you can start combining elements from them to form potential business or product ideas. For instance, if you enjoy conversing with others, have an interest in houseplants, and possess photography skills, you might explore opportunities like offering houseplant care classes, creating video tutorials on houseplant care, or selling photographs of houseplants.

Remember, you don't need to incorporate elements from all three categories—combining ideas from at least two can lead to innovative and personalized business concepts tailored to your preferences, interests, and skills.

Once you've generated several promising ideas, the next step is to rank them based on three key factors:

1. Excitement: Gauge your level of enthusiasm for each idea on a scale of 1 to 10. It's vital to choose a business that genuinely excites you, as the entrepreneurial journey requires dedication and motivation.

2. Value to Others: Assess how much value each idea would offer to potential customers, again using a 1 to 10 scale. Higher value often translates into the ability to charge higher prices and earn more.

3. Market Interest: Estimate the level of interest other people might have in your ideas. This step helps ensure there is a demand for your chosen business, making it easier to attract customers and generate revenue. Again, use a scale of 1 to 10 for ranking.

After completing this evaluation, there's one more exercise you can undertake to solidify your decision further: a visualization exercise. Imagine a typical day running each of these businesses, considering the type of work, effort, and demands they entail. This exercise will help you determine which business aligns best with your long-term goals and preferences.

Remember, there's no single correct answer when selecting a business idea. Many viable options may suit your personality and skills. The key is to choose one and start working on it. In a few months, you'll gain valuable insights into whether it's the right path for you or if you should pivot. Either way, you'll be ahead of where you are now.

SWOT Analysis: Navigating the Business Terrain

To chart your course effectively, you must conduct a SWOT analysis: an exploration of your strengths, weaknesses, opportunities, and threats. This critical evaluation offers a data-driven perspective on how your business concept might perform in the market.

Uncovering Strengths and Weaknesses: Delve into your business idea's strengths and weaknesses. Are there elements you haven't considered? Identifying these internal factors is vital for crafting a resilient strategy.

Exploring Opportunities and Threats: External factors also shape your business journey. By scrutinizing opportunities and threats, you can make informed decisions about the trajectory of your idea. Your analysis may reveal untapped potential or areas where you can outshine your competitors.

Here's a SWOT analysis table for Anthony, the plumber, to assess his strengths, weaknesses, opportunities, and threats as he starts his plumbing business:

Strengths (Internal)	Weaknesses (Internal)	Opportunities (External)	Threats (External)
. Plumbing xpertise	1. Limited Business Experience	1. Growing Local Market	1. Intense Local Competition
. Relevant ertifications	2. Initial Financial Constraints	2. Increasing Homeownership	2. Economic Downturn
. Exceptional ustomer Service	3. Limited Marketing Knowledge	3. Expanding Real Estate Market	3. Regulatory Changes
. Local nowledge	4. Limited Online Presence	4. High Demand for Plumbing Services	4. Seasonal Fluctuations
. Strong Work thic	5. Limited Networking	5. Partnerships with Local Businesses	5. Supply Chain Disruptions

This SWOT analysis serves as a valuable tool for Anthony to identify areas of focus and strategies to leverage his strengths, address weaknesses, seize opportunities, and mitigate potential threats as he establishes his plumbing business.

The R.O.I. concept and 4 Examples of viable businesses with less than $1,000

Let's dive into the concept of Return on Investment, affectionately known as ROI. It's the magic formula that can turn a small upfront investment into substantial returns. Picture this: You desire to pocket $10,000, and  you're willing to part with a mere $1,000. In this scenario, your ROI would be a staggering $9,000. Now that's what I call a financial victory.

But hold on, there's more to the story. We introduce another key metric called "investment length." It's all about the waiting game – how long it takes for your money to start rolling in. These two metrics, ROI and investment length, are the compasses we navigate when determining if a business venture is a golden opportunity.

Whenever you find yourself saying, "But I have no money," I implore you to revisit this chapter. We're about to unveil three business ideas that require less than a thousand dollars to kickstart. These aren't just whimsical theories; they're grounded in the real world of business. How do I know this? We've scrutinized hundreds of businesses each month, and we've not only invested in five of them but also partnered directly with three others. We aim to reveal the tangible truths of business.

Now, let's address the stock market, cryptocurrencies, and real estate. Stocks offer an average annual return of 10% over any ten years, translating to an ROI of 10%. However, it takes a year to make a hundred dollars on your thousand-dollar investment. Real estate fares slightly better with a 9.5% return on the high end, while single-family homes offer a meager 1.32%. So, on a thousand dollars invested, you're looking at an annual return ranging from $95 to $13. I own both stocks and real estate, and they're solid investments, but if you're working with a limited thousand-dollar budget, there might be a more promising path.

Enter the "Sell Matrix" – our secret sauce. It comprises four crucial characteristics that define a business worth pursuing:

1. Sellable: You can start selling a product from day one, with no need for a prolonged incubation period.

2. High Earning (E): These ventures have the potential to rake in over $100,000 in annual profit. No mere side hustles here.

3. Low Cost: Your initial investment should clock in at less than $1,000, making it accessible to budding entrepreneurs.

4. High Leverage: You can outsource a significant portion of the workload. Start the business, but you don't have to run it single-handedly forever.

But here's the catch: you must be willing to put in the work. Take the stairs, not the elevator. Conquer the challenges upfront, and you'll find that the cost of things becomes less of a concern. That's the trade-off we're talking about here.

Generating a business idea can seem daunting initially, but I'm here to simplify the process. I'll provide you with practical examples to demonstrate that any job can evolve into a business.

In the pages ahead, we'll explore how ordinary individuals have transformed their passions and skills into successful ventures. These real-life cases will inspire you and offer clarity on your path to discovering your entrepreneurial potential.

By the end, you'll see that the business world is open to anyone willing to explore their interests and seize opportunities. Let's dive in and uncover the potential hidden within your passions

Window Cleaning

Surprisingly, the window cleaning business fits this bill perfectly. Let's dive into the specifics.

Crunching the Numbers To kickstart your journey in the window cleaning industry, you'll need some basic equipment: $40 for accessories, $80 for a ladder, $40 for a hose, and $20 for a cleaning solution. These initial costs add up to around $180.

Profits Await Now, let's talk about profits. Window cleaning can be a highly lucrative venture. You can charge homeowners anywhere from $100 to $500 for window cleaning services. With just one or two clients, you not only cover your initial investment but potentially start earning. Scale up to five clients, and you're in the green. If you expand your services to include pressure washing, the income potential soars. The speaker even shares their experience of spending $2,500 on a fence pressure wash.

Outsourcing for Success The beauty of this business is that you don't have to be the one doing all the cleaning. Enter the concept of "employee arbitrage" or subcontracting. You generate leads and then subcontract the actual cleaning work to others in the industry who may struggle to find clients. Small cleaning business owners are often more than willing to accept these leads, and you can negotiate a percentage of the revenue generated from these subcontracted jobs.

Lessons from Mark's Playbook Let's take a real-world example: Mark, a 19-year-old entrepreneur, built a remote cleaning business that generated $20,000 per month. What's fascinating is the simplicity of his approach. He targeted large homes and businesses, charging them hundreds to thousands of dollars for window cleaning services.

Lead Generation Mastery One crucial aspect of Mark's success was his ability to secure new clients. He excelled in online advertising, using platforms like Google Ads, TikTok, Instagram, and local SEO to attract customers actively searching for cleaning services.

The Power of Employee Arbitrage Here's the game-changer: Mark didn't personally handle the cleaning. Instead, he leveraged employee arbitrage by providing leads to other small cleaning businesses in exchange for a share of the revenue. It's a win-win situation.

Scaling Up with Subcontractors Scaling this business involves finding reliable subcontractors. You can identify them through Google searches, local community groups, or industry trade associations. Assess their quality by examining their workload, reviews, pricing, experience, and customer referrals.

Why We Love This Business Model This window cleaning venture aligns with our finance model in several ways. It offers a high ROI, requires low initial investment, and can reach profitability within six months. Furthermore, it boasts low failure risk and bankruptcy risk, making it a safe and profitable choice.

Real Estate Video Editing

Real estate video editing presents such an opportunity, and let me share the compelling reasons why.

Unlocking the Potential You might be wondering, "But I'm not a video editor." Rest assured, you don't need to be. The beauty of this business lies in its simplicity—it's a process-driven game. Many shy away, assuming they can't edit, but I'm here to dispel that myth.

Simplicity in Complexity Creating captivating real estate videos may seem complex, but it's surprisingly straightforward. With just a few hours of effort, you can dive into this venture and discover the remarkable demand for your services.

Proof in Practice Consider the journey of my employee, Sam. He ventured into real estate video editing before I hired him. Initially, he shared the same apprehensions as many others. However, the simplicity of the process became evident as he delved deeper.

From Sam to Success In a matter of minutes, I watched Sam compile clips into stunning videos—something he had never done before. The result was a compelling visual narrative, akin to the work of a professional like.

Your Path to Profits Engaging in this business requires only a minimal time investment of two to three hours a day. Remarkably, Sam managed to generate an income of $100,000 annually, demonstrating the financial potential of this endeavor.

Meeting a Critical Need Real estate agents are in dire need of compelling video content for their property listings. Statistics reveal that listings with video content receive a staggering 403% more interest. Yet, a noticeable void exists in this market.

Seizing the Initiative Your journey begins by reaching out to real estate agents. Platforms like Zillow and Redfin provide easy access to their contact information. Personalize your approach by crafting specific emails, accompanied by sample videos.

Profitability Within Reach With as few as 20 clients paying $5,000 a month, you can find yourself on the path to earning hundreds of thousands of dollars annually. Samuel's success story attests to the viability of this business model.

Aligning with Financial Success Does this opportunity align with our financial model? Let's examine the metrics. First, it offers a high ROI, as evidenced by Samuel's substantial earnings. Second, it demands minimal initial investment, with a camera or even budget-friendly editing software being sufficient. Lastly, achieving profitability within six months is entirely feasible, with the potential for pre-orders within just 30 days.

Mobile car detailing

Have you ever noticed a flyer on your doorstep, promoting a mobile car detailing service? You might have shrugged it off initially, just like I did. However, a recent encounter with a young entrepreneur cleaning and detailing cars in my neighborhood opened my eyes to the hidden potential of this business. People are more than willing to pay top dollar for the convenience of mobile car detailing, and this chapter is your ticket to understanding how you can tap into this lucrative market.

Uncovering the Profit Potential

Surprisingly, there's a significant demand for car cleaning and detailing services. Many individuals are willing to pay for these services regularly, some even as often as once a month. The industry basts entrepreneurs who are raking in hundreds of dollars a day, thousands a week, and yes, even millions annually, all by making cars shine. The good news? Starting your own car detailing business is simpler than you might think.

The Road to Success

Let's break down the steps you need to take to jumpstart your journey into the world of mobile car detailing:

Step 1: Assess Your Finances

• Ensure you have a minimum of $150 available for your startup.

Step 2: Equip Yourself

• Make a trip to your local hardware store or Walmart. Pick up the essentials: a garden hose, a garden hose nozzle, a bucket, microfiber towels, glass cleaner, auto cleaner, a wash mitt, detailing brushes, tire-cleaning tools, a tire shiner, an extension cord, and a shop vac.

• You'll need access to running water and electricity since you'll be operating as a mobile auto cleaner. You can either invest in a 15 to 25-gallon water tank (ranging from $100 to $200) and a portable power station (around $140) or seek permission from homeowners to connect to their outdoor water and power sources.

Step 3: Find Clients

• To get started, you'll need customers. Leverage free platforms like Facebook Marketplace, local Facebook groups, Craigslist, and Nextdoor to promote your services.

• Consider investing in door-hanging flyers. You can purchase 1,000 of these for approximately 13 cents each through services like Vistaprint. Buying in bulk will save you money.

• Focus your efforts on distributing flyers in upscale, affluent neighborhoods to attract high-end clients.

Calculating Your Earnings Potential

Let's crunch some numbers to give you an idea of your potential earnings. Suppose you charge between $50 and $100 for a single car detailing session, and you manage to clean five cars over four to five hours, six days a week. This translates to an average weekly income ranging from $1,500 to $3,000, or $6,000 to $12,000 per month. That's not just a boost to your bank account; it's a life-changing opportunity.

Lawn care

Starting your own business and becoming your own boss can seem like a daunting endeavor, often overly complicated and filled with uncertainties. People around you, whether friends or family, may dismiss your ambitions, claiming it's not as easy as it sounds. However, I'm here to tell you, as someone who hasn't had a boss for nearly a decade, it can be that straightforward, especially when it comes to a lawn care business.

Unlocking the Lawn Care Opportunity

Lawn care is a thriving industry, valued at a staggering $129 billion, and it continues to expand year after year. The beauty of this business lies in its simplicity and accessibility. You don't need much to get started, making it an ideal choice for aspiring entrepreneurs. So, let's break down the essentials you'll need:

Step 1: Acquire the Basics

• The cornerstone of your lawn care venture is undoubtedly a lawnmower. Now, here's where misconceptions often creep in. Do you need to splurge on a $2,000 or $3,000 zero-turn or riding lawnmower to kickstart your business? Not necessarily. Your budget and goals will play a role, but it's essential to understand that you can establish a thriving lawn care business with just a few key tools.

• Start with a push mower, which can be obtained for as little as $200 to $400.

• Equip yourself with a budget-friendly hedge trimmer, a leaf blower, and a cost-effective weed whacker (or weed eater, depending on your region).

Step 2: Keep It Simple

• The testimony of countless successful lawn care entrepreneurs proves that you don't need an extensive arsenal of equipment to achieve remarkable results. Below $500, you can potentially earn $500. Simplicity is key.

• Consider my setup, for instance: a mower, a trimmer, and a blower. It's a testament to the fact that you don't need much to achieve a lot.

• This business is a testament to the power of self-reliance and taking control of your financial destiny.

These examples highlight the potential for turning a skill or passion into a successful business. Entrepreneurship is not limited to specific industries or predefined paths. Any job or skill can become the foundation of a business venture if you have the know-how, determination, and a solid business plan.

The key is to identify what you enjoy doing or excel at and then explore how to leverage that expertise to create a thriving business. Whether it's a service, a product, or a unique combination of both, there are countless opportunities to turn your passion or skill into a successful venture.

Chapter 3: Crafting a Business Plan, Your Roadmap to Success

*H*aving a solid business plan is of  paramount importance because it can save you from squandering your valuable time and financial resources. Countless individuals face failure in their entrepreneurial pursuits because they dive headfirst into new business ventures without a well-thought-out plan. Eventually, they realize that they lack a genuine competitive edge or a product-market fit. Crafting a comprehensive business plan compels you to scrutinize your business concepts, assess various strategies, and consider how to establish a presence in the marketplace. It also prompts you to assemble the right team, whether through attracting investors, securing partners, or recruiting essential talent.

Before launching your business, I strongly recommend dedicating time to developing a well-crafted business plan. By doing so, you can seek input and feedback from trusted advisors, mentors, consultants, or your local SBDC (Small Business Development Center). However, the first step is to create a formidable plan.

In this chapter, we will explore the three types of business plans you can create and guide you through the step-by-step process of crafting an effective one.

Business Plan Definition

A business plan is a detailed documentation that provides an exhaustive outline of your financial goals. It details the fundamentals of your financial efforts, including their nature, revenue-generating methods, leadership and staffing plans, financing schemes, operational frameworks, and a wide range of other intricate details that support their performance. A well-structured business plan extends beyond the financial realm; it encompasses a marketing strategy, a mission statement, and the cherished values that define your financial journey.

It is imperative to recognize that, in many instances, financial institutions and potential investors will demand sight of your business plan as a prerequisite for financial backing. However, even if external funding is not on your horizon, a meticulously curated plan serves as the North Star guiding your financial enterprise as it navigates the ever-evolving landscape of personal finance.

The prospect of an empty page can be overwhelming, often instilling a sense of trepidation. Yet, embarking on the journey of crafting a business plan can be greatly facilitated by initiating it with a well-defined structure and predefined elements for each section. To this end, we offer a structured outline—a foundational scaffold—to commence your business plan creation, sparing you the anxiety of confronting an unfilled canvas. Additionally, we recommend commencing with a readily available business plan template, which can seamlessly guide the organization and composition of your plan.

With the framework in place, your next step is to breathe life into it. We have methodically divided this process into sections to facilitate a systematic, step-by-step approach to constructing your financial blueprint.

The Three Types of Business Plans

Business plans come in various formats, depending on your specific objectives. Let's discuss the three common types:

1. Traditional Business Plan: This format is the most comprehensive, typically spanning six to seven sections, including an executive summary and financial projections. It's the go-to choice when seeking funding from banks or venture capital firms.

2. Lean Business Plan: A simplified business plan more condensed than the standard version and can often fit on a single page. It serves well when onboarding key team members or for personal use.

3. Non-Profit Plan: Similar to a traditional plan, this format includes detailed information about how your organization will make a positive impact on society.

Now that you understand the types of business plans, let's dive into the step-by-step process of crafting one. Your business plan should encompass these core sections:

1. Compose an Executive Summary

2. Company Description

3. Market Analysis

4. Management and Organizational Structure

5. Products and Services

6. Customer Segmentation

7. Marketing

8. Financial Blueprint

1. Compose an Executive Summary

The fundamental purpose of the executive summary is to distill the entirety of your subsequent content, offering time-sensitive reviewers, such as potential investors and lenders, a high-level glimpse into your financial blueprint. This succinct yet compelling summary should motivate them to delve deeper into the document.

It's essential to remember that this is a summary—thus, your task is to spotlight the critical insights uncovered during the crafting of your financial plan. If you're assembling this plan for your financial strategy, you may consider bypassing the summary section. However, it is advisable to indulge in the exercise, even if solely for practice.

An executive summary should be concise, ideally limited to a single page. While this space constraint may seem daunting, it's entirely feasible to encapsulate all pertinent information effectively. Your business plan's executive summary should encompass:

• Business Concept: A concise depiction of your financial pursuits.

• Business Goals and Vision: An articulation of your financial aspirations.

• Product Description and Uniqueness: Details on your financial offerings and what sets them apart.

• Target Market: An identification of your clientele.

• Marketing Strategy: Insights into your customer outreach tactics.

• Current Financial State: A snapshot of your existing revenue.

• Projected Financial State: Forecasts for future revenue.

• The Funding Request: The financial resources you are seeking.

• The Team: An introduction to the individuals involved in your financial endeavors.

2. Write a Company Description

Two key questions are addressed in this part of your financial plan: Who are you and what are your financial goals?

By providing a comprehensive company description, you introduce the essence of your financial pursuits, elucidating why your financial journey has commenced, what distinguishes you from others, your unique strengths, and the reasons for considering your venture a wise investment.

For instance, the clean makeup brand, Saie, articulates its mission and the rationale behind its existence through a heartfelt letter from its founder.

The company description endeavor remains valuable, even if you are the sole audience. It is an opportunity to articulate the intangible aspects of your financial undertaking, including your principles, ideals, and cultural philosophies.

Components to be incorporated within your company description encompass:

• Business Structure: Your legal business entity (e.g., general partnership, limited partnership, sole proprietorship, or incorporated company).

• Business Model: A delineation of your financial framework.

• Industry Analysis: A comprehensive overview of your industry.

• Vision, Mission, and Value Proposition: The guiding principles that underpin your financial journey.

• Background Information: Pertinent historical context related to your financial venture.

• Business Objectives: Short and long-term financial objectives.

• The Team: A profile of key personnel and their remuneration.

• Brand Objectives and Values: Core values and financial aspirations.

Understand your responsibility to multiple stakeholders, like as owners, employees, suppliers, customers, and investors as you create your brand values. Think about the interaction you want to have with each of these entities. Your main values ought to become clear after doing this analysis.

Additionally, both your company's short-term and long-term financial objectives should be stated in the description. Long-term goals should have a time horizon of one to five years, whereas short-term targets should be achievable within the next year. Make sure your goals are specific, measurable, attained, realistic, and time-bound (SMART).

After this task, a vision and mission statement should be created. Your mission statement, which should normally be no more than one phrase, should be an engaging, succinct articulation of why your business exists. Create your vision statement after that, imagining the effect your business will have on the world once it is accomplished. Start off your description of this vision by saying, "We will." While vision statements may contain more than one sentence, make an effort to keep them brief—ideally, they should not exceed three sentences.

3. Conduct a Market Analysis

Regardless of the nature of your financial undertaking, it is unequivocal that your chosen market can be the ultimate arbiter of your success. Opt for a market that aligns with your financial products— one characterized by a robust customer base that comprehends and requires your offerings— and you gain a competitive edge. Conversely, an ill-timed choice can result in arduous sales endeavors.

Hence, market research and analysis assume pivotal roles within your financial plan, whether intended for external readers or your personal use alone.

This important part demands an explanation of the estimated size of your financial organization's market for its products, an analysis of the market positioning of that enterprise, and a summary of the competition environment. In order to successfully navigate your financial path, you need solid research to support your conclusions, convince investors, and validate your assumptions.

While envisioning soaring sales figures can be exhilarating, it is imperative to substantiate your projected market size with relevant, impartial data.

As this undertaking may appear formidable, here are some general guidelines to initiate your research:

Here are some general suggestions to help you start your investigation because this project may seem challenging:

1. Establish the profile of your ideal client: Knowing your target consumer profile is a good place to start. Look for government sites that can provide you with information about the sociodemographics, geographic areas, preferred social networks, and purchasing patterns of your target market.

2. Explore Industry Trends: Investigate pertinent industry trends and trajectories. Analyze consumer preferences and emerging product trends within your sector. Platforms like Google Trends, trade publications, and influential figures in your industry can provide valuable insights.

3.   Informed Estimations: It is essential to acknowledge that attaining comprehensive and perfect information about your total addressable market is an elusive goal. Your objective should be to base your estimations on a foundation of verifiable data points and informed assessments.

Consider consulting sources like government statistics agencies, business groups, academic research publications, and reliable news organizations that specialize in your industry when acquiring market data.

Performing a SWOT Examination

As we have already seen in the previous chapter, a SWOT analysis serves as a robust tool for evaluating your financial enterprise's internal strengths and weaknesses, alongside external opportunities and threats.

To embark on a SWOT analysis, examine the following aspects:

• Strengths: Identify the key strengths that set your financial company apart. These could encompass unique offerings, exceptional expertise, or proprietary technology.

• Weaknesses: Confront your company's limitations and areas that require enhancement. Acknowledge any deficiencies that may hinder your competitiveness.

• Opportunities: Delve into the market and industry dynamics to uncover potential opportunities for growth and advancement. Explore avenues where your financial products or services can excel.

• Threats: Assess external factors that pose risks to your company's success. Recognize elements that could potentially impede your progress or market penetration.

If you have not already done so, develop a SWOT following the directions in the previous chapter, then incorporate it into your business plan.

4. Establishing Your Management and Organizational Structure

In the management and organization segment of your financial blueprint, it becomes paramount to acquaint readers with the individuals steering the helm of your financial enterprise. Here, you will delve into the legal framework underpinning your business, specifying whether it will adopt the form of an S corporation, limited partnership, sole proprietorship, or another legal structure.

Should you possess a dedicated management team, consider employing an organizational chart as a visual aid, elucidating the internal structure of your company. This chart should encompass roles, responsibilities, and the interrelationships among personnel, outlining how each individual contributes to the success of your startup.

5. Cataloging Your Products and Services

The products or services you offer serve as central components of your financial plan, warranting a dedicated section that furnishes key insights for interested readers.

If your product catalog is extensive, it is acceptable to furnish general information about each product line. However, in the case of a limited product range, delve deeper into the specifics of each offering. For instance, consider the example of Baggu, a bag shop offering various bag types alongside home goods and accessories. Their business plan would necessitate outlining these categories and furnishing essential product details.

Additionally, introduce forthcoming products in the pipeline and any intellectual property holdings, expounding upon how these elements are poised to enhance profitability. Highlight the sourcing of products as well, as they vary significantly, ranging from handmade crafts to trending dropshipping items.

6. Conduction of Customer Segmentation

Your ideal customer, often referred to as your target market, forms the bedrock of your marketing strategy and, indeed, your entire financial plan. Therefore, it is imperative to provide a comprehensive overview of this quintessential audience within your blueprint.

To comprehensively define your ideal customer, elaborate on a range of demographic attributes, encompassing:

• Geographic locations

• Age demographics

• Educational levels

• Behavioral patterns

• Leisure activities

• Employment particulars

• Technological preferences

• Income brackets

• Common workplaces

• Values, beliefs, or viewpoints

The specifics of this delineation may vary based on the nature of your financial offerings. Nevertheless, precision should prevail, ensuring absolute clarity regarding your target audience and the rationale behind your strategic choices, aligning with their preferences and values.

For instance, the interests, shopping behaviors, and price sensitivity of a college student significantly differ from those of a 50-year-old executive at a Fortune 500 company. Consequently, your financial plan and decisions would inherently diverge depending on which demographic represents your ideal customer.

7. Defining Your Marketing Blueprint

Your marketing endeavors derive direct inspiration from your ideal customer. The marketing plan segment should expound upon your current strategies and future strategies, with a particular emphasis on how your financial concept aligns with your ideal customer.

For instance, if you intend to heavily invest in Instagram or TikTok marketing, it is prudent to consider whether these platforms resonate with your target audience. If not, this incongruence may necessitate a reevaluation of your marketing blueprint.

Most marketing plans encompass four primary areas, with the level of detail contingent upon both your business and the intended audience of your plan:

• Price: Delve into the pricing of your products or services, elucidating the rationale behind your pricing decisions.

• Product: Elaborate on the nature of your offerings and articulate the differentiating factors that set them apart in the market.

• Promotion: Detail your strategies for product exposure to your ideal customer, encompassing the channels and markets you intend to explore.

• Place: Define your distribution channels and markets, disclosing where your products will be available.

While the promotion aspect may command more attention due to its tactical nature, the other three elements should receive at least a cursory mention, as each wields strategic significance within your marketing mix.

8. Furnishing a Logistics and Operations Strategy

Logistics and operations constitute the procedural frameworks that will actualize your financial vision. Even if your business plan is for personal use, this section merits consideration, albeit potentially requiring less granular detail compared to a plan intended for external stakeholders.

Encompass all facets of your planned operations, encompassing:

• Suppliers: Disclose the sources of your raw materials or products and delineate the logistics of production or sourcing.

• Production: Specify whether you will manufacture, wholesale, dropship, or undertake other production methods. Address production timeframes and contingency plans for fluctuating demand.

• Facilities: Clarify the locations where you and your team will operate, elucidating whether physical retail spaces are part of your strategy.

• Equipment: Detail the technological and equipment requirements essential for your operations.

• Shipping and Fulfillment: Address how fulfillment tasks will be managed—whether in-house or through third-party partners.

• Inventory: Specify the inventory volume and storage locations, and elaborate on your inventory management strategies.

This section serves as an indicator to your reader that you possess a comprehensive grasp of your supply chain and are equipped with robust contingency plans to navigate potential uncertainties.

9. Crafting a Financial Blueprint

Regardless of the brilliance of your concept, the fate of your financial enterprise hinges on its fiscal health. Ultimately, people gravitate towards businesses they deem sustainable in the long run.

The audience and objectives you have in mind will determine the level of details in your financial plan. However, generally speaking, you should take into account the income statement, the balance sheet, and the cash-flow statement as the three main financial viewpoints. It could also be important to incorporate financial information and estimates.

The types of financial statements you need to include are explained in the following:

• Earnings Statements: This statement provides a thorough overview of your sources of income and outlays over a given time period. It offers information on the profits or losses your company had throughout that time. You might make projections for future revenue milestones for startups.

• Balance Sheets: The balance sheet offers a snapshot of your business's equity. It juxtaposes assets (what you own) against liabilities (what you owe) to determine shareholder equity, defined as Assets - Liabilities = Equity.

• Cash Flow Statements: Similar to an income statement, this document accounts for revenue collection and expense payments. It discloses whether your cash flow is positive or negative based on the balance between incoming and outgoing cash. Forecasting your cash-flow statement can pinpoint gaps or negative cash flow, prompting necessary operational adjustments.

Here is a very concise example of the business plan that Anthony the plumber created at the beginning of his business and then developed and improved over time:

1. Executive Summary

Business Concept: Anthony the Plumber is a plumbing service company dedicated to providing high-quality plumbing solutions to residential and commercial clients. Our mission is to offer reliable, efficient, and cost-effective plumbing services, ensuring customer satisfaction while maintaining the highest standards of professionalism.

Business Goals and Vision: To become a trusted name in the plumbing industry within our region, providing top-notch plumbing services to our clients, expanding our customer base, and maintaining a profitable and sustainable business.

The Ask: We are seeking a startup capital investment of $50,000 to cover initial expenses, marketing, and working capital.

2. Company Description

Business Structure: Anthony the Plumber operates as a Limited Liability Company (LLC).

Business Model: We operate on a service-based model, charging clients for plumbing services rendered.

Industry: Plumbing Services

Vision, Mission, and Value Proposition:

• Mission: To provide reliable plumbing solutions that exceed customer expectations.

• Vision: To be the go-to plumbing service provider in our region, recognized for excellence and integrity.

• Value Proposition: Quality work, prompt response, and fair pricing.

Business Objectives: Establish a strong local presence, build a loyal customer base, expand our service area, diversify offerings, and achieve sustained profitability.

3. Market Analysis

Potential Market: We target both residential and commercial clients within our service area, including homeowners, property managers, and businesses.

Demographic Characteristics: Varied age groups and occupations seeking prompt and efficient plumbing solutions.

Behavior Patterns: Value quality work, professionalism, and responsiveness from local service providers.

4. Management and Organization

Legal Structure: Anthony the Plumber is an LLC.

Management Team:

• Anthony Smith, Founder and Master Plumber

• Sarah Johnson, Operations Manager

Organizational Chart: We have a streamlined internal structure to ensure efficient operations.

5. Products and Services

Services Offered:

• Plumbing Repairs

• Plumbing Installations

• Maintenance Contracts

• Emergency Plumbing Services

Product Innovation: We continuously explore advanced plumbing technologies to enhance our service offerings.

6. Customer Segmentation

Ideal Customer Profile: Homeowners, property managers, and business owners in need of reliable plumbing services within our service area.

Demographic Characteristics: Varied age, occupation, and location within our service area.

Behavior Patterns: Seek prompt and efficient plumbing solutions, value quality work, and professionalism.

7. Marketing Plan

Marketing Channels:

• Website and Online Presence

• Social Media Advertising

• Local SEO

• Community Engagement

Price Strategy: Competitive pricing based on industry standards, transparently communicated to clients.

Product Strategy: Highlight our comprehensive plumbing services and reliability in marketing materials.

Promotion: Offer promotions for first-time customers and referral incentives.

Place: Focused on local marketing efforts within our service area.

8. Logistics and Operations Plan

Suppliers: We source plumbing materials and equipment from reputable suppliers to ensure quality.

Production: Efficient scheduling and timely responses to service requests are our priorities.

Facilities: Our operations are based in [Specify Location]. We do not maintain a physical storefront at this time.

Equipment: We utilize state-of-the-art plumbing tools and equipment.

Shipping and Fulfillment: Our services are on-site, eliminating the need for shipping or fulfillment.

Inventory: We maintain an inventory of essential plumbing components.

9. Financial Plan

Income Statement: Projected revenue growth over the first three years, including forecasted expenses.

Balance Sheet: Assets, including equipment and working capital, and liabilities if any.

Cash Flow Statement: Cash inflow and outflow projections, along with contingency plans for managing cash flow.

Financial Projections: Anticipate breaking even within the first year and achieving steady profitability thereafter.

Utilize Business Planning Software Solutions

Writing a comprehensive business plan can pose a formidable challenge for entrepreneurs. However, it remains a vital endeavor for individuals embarking on new ventures or seeking to expand their existing businesses. Fortunately, a plethora of tools are at your disposal to streamline this process, encompassing tasks such as planning, drafting, graphic design, integrating financial data, and more. Business planning software packages also offer a wide array of templates and tutorials to expedite the creation of a comprehensive plan, reducing the time investment from days to mere hours.

Some carefully selected options include:

• LivePlan: Positioned as the most cost-effective choice, LivePlan provides an abundance of samples and templates.

• Bizplan: Tailored to cater to the unique needs of startups actively seeking investment.

• Go Small Biz: A budget-friendly solution featuring industry-specific templates.

For more information: Delve deeper into the subject with our comprehensive article on the "6 Best Business Planning Software Tools to Streamline Your Planning Process."

Common Mistakes to Avoid When Crafting Your Business Plan

In contrast to many other resources on the topic of business plans, we acknowledge a critical reality: a business plan can indeed falter. The last scenario any entrepreneur desires is for their time and effort to be rendered futile. To mitigate this risk, steer clear of the following common missteps:

• Ill-Conceived Business Idea: Occasionally, your business concept may prove excessively precarious for potential investors, financially unsustainable, or bereft of a viable market. Aim for small business concepts that entail minimal startup costs.

• Lack of Exit Strategy: Failing to furnish an exit strategy or a plan for investors to depart the business while maximizing returns, will significantly impede your efforts to secure capital.

• Imbalanced Teams: While a remarkable product is a fundamental prerequisite for initiating a business, an exceptional team can elevate it to unprecedented heights. Regrettably, many business proprietors overlook the importance of assembling a well-rounded team, focusing solely on potential profits without due consideration for execution.

• Omission of Financial Projections: Do not overlook the inclusion of crucial financial documents, including balance sheets, cash flow statements, profit and loss statements, income statements, break-even analyses, and return-on-investment calculations. These elements collectively form the cornerstone of a prosperous business plan.

• Spelling and Grammar Errors: The most esteemed organizations invariably enlist the services of an editor to meticulously review their documents. Should a reader encounter typographical errors while perusing your business plan, doubts may arise regarding your ability to manage a successful enterprise.

Commence Your Business Plan Today

A meticulously crafted business plan serves as a compass, guiding your enterprise toward deliberate and discernible milestones, even if you have no intentions of courting investors. Furthermore, it offers the invaluable capacity to identify potential weaknesses within your plan before they evolve into critical issues

Chapter 4: Start a Business with Zero Budget

*A*s budding entrepreneurs embark on the journey of establishing a new business, the foremost hurdle they encounter is securing the necessary capital. Nevertheless, each year, a substantial number of determined individuals manage to surmount this financial obstacle and successfully initiate their ventures. The question then arises: How do they accomplish this feat, and, more significantly, how can you procure funds for your nascent enterprise?

Herein, we proffer sagacious counsel to facilitate the acquisition of funding essential for the auspicious commencement of your entrepreneurial endeavor:

1. Leverage Personal Savings: Your initial recourse when seeking financial support for your business should be your reservoir of savings. Depending on the capital required to inaugurate your enterprise, you may tap into your personal savings, an inheritance, or a portion of your disposable income. It is imperative, however, to ensure that the funds you allocate are genuinely "disposable." The inherent risk of business failure necessitates prudence; thus, it is inadvisable to invest retirement savings or funds earmarked for future necessities. Furthermore, maintain a financial buffer to address unforeseen contingencies such as unexpected car repairs or other exigencies. Additionally, mitigating risk involves dedicating time to acquaint yourself with the proper protocols for launching a business.

2. Embrace Frugality to Fuel Your Business: You have the potential to accumulate a portion of your startup capital by judiciously trimming personal expenditures. While it may necessitate patience, frugality need not entail austere living or the exhaustive pursuit of trivial savings. Even modest lifestyle modifications can yield substantial monthly savings. For instance, one astute journalist documented her monthly expenditures on restaurant meals and premium coffee, revealing a staggering total of $645.75. By simply substituting homemade coffee for expensive cafe purchases or

bringing packed lunches to work instead of ordering out, you could realize savings of $10 to $15 per week. Moreover, transitioning from restaurant dining to home-cooked meals not only conserves funds but also potentially saves an additional $20 to $30 weekly, along with any tips typically extended to delivery services. Economizing on utilities by modestly adjusting your thermostat during heating and cooling seasons can result in notable annual savings. Furthermore, curtailing impulsive spending and unnecessary purchases can contribute further to your financial reservoir.

3. Commence Part-Time: If your financial obligations mandate a stable income stream (including maintaining health insurance coverage for your family), consider launching your business as a part-time endeavor. It is prudent to refrain from relinquishing your primary source of income until your part-time business garners a consistent clientele and generates profits commensurate with your needs.

4. Pursue Used Equipment: While the allure of brand-new equipment, furnishings, and office accouterments is undeniable, considerable savings may be achieved by procuring essential items secondhand. Conduct comprehensive online searches for "used restaurant equipment," "used laboratory apparatus," or "used office furniture." Peruse listings on Craigslist and peruse local newspapers for notices of businesses liquidating assets. Additionally, garage sales and relocation sales in your vicinity may yield economical acquisitions to equip your enterprise.

5. Explore SBA-Guaranteed Loans: In the event your bank declines your business loan application, inquire about the possibility of an SBA-guaranteed loan. Should your bank consent, they will forward your loan request and credit information to the nearest SBA district office for evaluation and adjudication.

6. Seek Assistance from Family and Friends: Family members and close friends often serve as a viable source of initial funding for small business startups. However, exercise prudence in this

endeavor. Do not approach them for financial support unless you have meticulously devised a comprehensive business plan and conducted diligent market research to validate the demand for your offerings. Furthermore, ensure your financial arrangements encompass mechanisms for interest repayment on loans extended by family and friends.

7. Engage Angel Investors: Angel investors are prospective benefactors who furnish capital to nascent businesses in exchange for convertible debt or ownership equity. Notably, several renowned tech giants, including Google and Yahoo, were nurtured by angel investors. If your business exhibits signs of growth and potential, pursuing angel investors can be a viable avenue for securing funding.

8. Consider Venture Capitalists: Venture capitalists, akin to angel investors, extend financial backing to startups, early-stage enterprises, and burgeoning companies with substantial growth prospects. The distinction lies in their inclination toward investments yielding higher returns as opposed to claiming a share of company ownership. Nevertheless, some venture capitalists may opt for an ownership stake in the enterprise.

9. Consider starting some hide hustles: Side hustles can be very convenient to combine with your current job in order to create capital and start your own business.

- Participate in Paid Surveys: Engaging in online surveys via platforms like Swagbucks and Branded Surveys offers a straightforward way to earn extra cash. While the income may not be substantial, consistent participation can yield decent returns.

- Offer Pet-Sitting Services: The burgeoning pet-sitting industry, facilitated by platforms like Rover and PetBacker, presents a promising avenue for animal enthusiasts. Certification from organizations like Pet Sitters International enhances credibility and pet-sitting insurance safeguards against liabilities.

- Sell Stock Images or Music: Creative individuals can monetize their photography and music compositions by selling them on microstock websites like Shutterstock and TunePocket. Consistency and an understanding of market trends are essential for success.

- Be a Rideshare Driver and Do Deliveries: Those with access to a vehicle can explore the opportunity of being a rideshare driver or a delivery courier through platforms like Uber, Lyft, Postmates, or DoorDash. Earnings can vary based on location, working hours, and tips.

- Flip Items for Profit: Item flipping involves sourcing and reselling goods at a profit, often from thrift stores or garage sales. This scalable venture demands keen attention to product quality, pricing, and market trends, with potential earnings ranging from $500 to $3,000 per month in the first year.

- Get Paid to Review Books: Book enthusiasts can monetize their passion by becoming book reviewers. Websites like Online Book Club, Kirkus Media, and Women's Review of Books offer opportunities, with an average hourly rate of approximately $21.

- Take up Handyperson Jobs: Skilled individuals can offer handyperson services, and advertising through local publications, social media, or platforms like Craigslist and Porch. Earnings average around $44,000 per year.

- Accept Drawing or Graphic Design Commissions: Those with artistic talents can explore graphic design and illustration commissions. Building a portfolio and joining design marketplaces like 99designs or Minty can lead to earnings that vary based on experience and project size, with an estimated average of $48,000 per year.

Start a business online: Here's a list of some of the best online business ideas that require minimal to no upfront investment:

1. Freelancing: Offer your skills as a freelance writer, graphic designer, web developer, or social media manager. Platforms like Upwork, Fiverr, and Freelancer can help you find clients.

2. Content Creation: Start a blog, YouTube channel, or podcast and monetize it through ads, sponsorships, or affiliate marketing.

3. Dropshipping: Create an e-commerce store and partner with suppliers to sell their products online without holding inventory. Platforms like Shopify can help you get started.

4. Print on Demand: Design custom T-shirts, mugs, or other merchandise and sell them through platforms like Printful or Teespring.

5. Affiliate Marketing: Promote products or services on your website or social media and earn commissions for each sale or lead generated through your referral.

6. Online Consulting/Coaching: Offer your expertise in areas like business, fitness, or personal development through virtual coaching sessions or consultations.

7. Online Tutoring: If you know a particular subject, you can tutor students online through platforms like VIPKid or Chegg Tutors.

8. Virtual Assistant: Provide administrative support services to businesses or entrepreneurs remotely.

9. Sell Digital Products: Create and sell digital products like ebooks, online courses, printables, or stock photos on platforms like Gumroad or Etsy.

10. Social Media Management: Manage social media accounts for businesses to help them grow their online presence.

11. E-book Publishing: Write and self-publish ebooks on platforms like Amazon Kindle Direct Publishing.

12. Online Art and Crafts Sales: Sell your handmade crafts, artwork, or vintage items on platforms like Etsy.

Chapter 5: Choose the best entity structure for your business

Now, I want to discuss how to select the optimal legal structure for your business. At this moment, you might be pondering, "Hey, what's the distinction between an LLC and an S. Corp or a Schedule C., and how do I make a choice?" This chapter is going to be

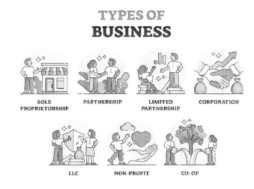

highly beneficial for anyone embarking on a new business venture or even for those with an established business that has changed over time. You might find yourself in a situation where you wish to revisit and enhance your business entity structure. In this chapter, I aim to address the significance of making the right entity choice, provide an overview of the four primary types and subtypes of business structures, and simplify the selection process based on your business objectives.

What Is a Business Entity?

Let's begin with something straightforward and progressively delve into more advanced topics. Starting with the basics: what precisely is a business entity or legal structure? The simplest way to define a business entity is as the framework within which you conduct business activities, including the sale of goods and services. Therefore, choosing your business entity is a crucial decision when launching a new business. If you don't actively select your business entity, you typically default to either a sole proprietorship or a general partnership, which isn't necessarily unfavorable. It's worth noting that you can change your business entity later or opt for a different tax treatment, as we'll discuss later in this chapter.

A common misconception is that a specific business structure is necessary to claim business expense deductions. This is not accurate. Regardless of whether you identify as a self-employed business owner, you can avail of similar tax deductions for a sole proprietorship, LLC, or S Corporation. In general, to establish a business entity structure, you need to register your business with the Secretary of State, verify the availability of your business name within the state, list all business partners or members, select your entity type, designate a registered agent for receiving correspondence, pay a nominal registration fee, and your business will be officially established.

Why Choosing the Right Business Structure Matters

Now that you understand what a business entity is, let's explore why selecting the appropriate business entity is of utmost importance.

Three key factors come into play when deciding how to structure your company:

• Legal protections provided by the entity

• Tax treatment and potential tax outcomes

• Level of government requirements associated with the chosen entity.

This decision can be likened to solving a puzzle, as making the wrong choice might expose your personal assets to risk, result in unnecessary tax liabilities, or entail government obligations that hinder your business growth. Therefore, your selection should be made wisely to ensure the most favorable outcomes. If you require assistance with tax planning, there are a few remaining appointments available, both with me and my father, who is also involved in the business. However, please note that our availability is limited as the tax season is nearly concluded. Feel free to click the first link in the description below if you require further assistance today.

Sole Proprietorships

Let's proceed, where we'll break down the four categories of business entities. Business entities can be neatly categorized into four types: sole proprietorships, partnerships, corporations, and LLCs. Let's embark on an in-depth exploration of each, starting with the first chapter of our discussion, "Sole Proprietorships."

A sole proprietorship stands out as the most straightforward business entity. In fact, according to the law, if you initiate a new business venture and are its sole owner, you automatically assume the status of a sole proprietor. This means you do not need to engage with your state's secretary of state or complete any paperwork. However, it's worth noting that certain states may require you to obtain a local business license or permit to sell specific goods or services.

Typically, individuals who identify as freelancers, consultants, delivery drivers, independent contractors, and other service professionals operate as sole proprietors. This explains why it is the most common business structure. Some individuals may not even realize they are establishing a business and becoming sole proprietors by default when setting up side hustles or side gigs.

The advantages of a sole proprietorship are evident. It is easy to establish since there is no need for formal state registration, and government paperwork or ongoing requirements are minimal. Moreover, you can still claim qualified business tax deductions, and filing your taxes remains relatively uncomplicated and cost-effective.

However, there are significant drawbacks to consider. The most substantial disadvantage is the absence of legal liability protection.

As a sole proprietor, you bear personal responsibility for all the business's debts and liabilities. In the event of a lawsuit against your business, creditors may attempt to seize your personal assets, including your car, home, or personal bank accounts.

Another noteworthy disadvantage is the challenge of building business credit. Due to the lack of legal separation between you and your business, lenders may find it challenging to assess your personal and business financial standing comprehensively. This difficulty in building business credit can hamper your ability to secure financing or loans for your new venture.

In light of these considerations, it's crucial to weigh the pros and cons carefully before deciding whether a sole proprietorship is the right choice for your business endeavors.

Pros:

• Easy setup.

• Minimal government requirements.

• Eligible for business tax deductions.

• Full control over business decisions.

• Direct ownership of profits.

• Flexibility in management.

• Lower startup costs.

Cons:

• No legal liability protection.

• Personal responsibility for debts.

• Risk of asset seizure in lawsuits.

• Difficulty building business credit.

• Limited access to capital.

• Sole responsibility for business operations.

General Partnerships

As we continue our journey through the landscape of business entities, we arrive where we delve into the intricacies of the General Partnership (GP). In many ways, the General Partnership bears a striking resemblance to its solitary counterpart, the Sole Proprietorship. The key distinction lies in the number of owners, for instead of a lone entrepreneur, a General Partnership features two or more co-owners. Under the legal framework, the presence of two or more owners automatically classifies the business as a General Partnership.

Much like its solitary counterpart, setting up a General Partnership is relatively uncomplicated, with no onerous paperwork requirements – although it's prudent to establish a robust partnership agreement. In terms of tax benefits, a General Partnership shares the same advantages as a Sole Proprietorship and other business entities. However, there's a unique pro worth noting here: the distribution of personal and business risks. With a partner by your side, you're no longer bearing the brunt of challenges alone. Legal matters, business losses, and responsibilities are shared, mitigating the burden placed on a single individual.

Nevertheless, the substantial con of legal liability remains a stark reality in the realm of General Partnerships. The exposure of personal assets to potential lawsuits persists. Furthermore, having a partner also entails shared control and the potential for internal disputes. Divergent visions and conflicting perspectives could stifle business progress, emphasizing the importance of a well-crafted partnership agreement.

On the subject of taxes, it's worth noting that General Partnerships require separate tax returns, which can be perceived as a minor drawback. Lastly, even after overcoming these challenges, you must still share profits with your partner. This dynamic presents both opportunities and considerations that must be carefully weighed as you navigate the intricate world of business entities.

Pros:

• Relatively simple setup, akin to Sole Proprietorships.

• No extensive paperwork is required, although a well-structured partnership agreement is advisable.

• Enjoy tax advantages similar to Sole Proprietorships and other business entities.

• Shared responsibility for personal and business risks, lightening the load on individual partners.

• Potential for collaborative problem-solving and support.

• A flexible business structure that allows for multiple owners.

Cons:

• Substantial legal liability, risking personal assets in the event of lawsuits.

• Shared control may lead to internal disputes and hinder decision-making.

• Divergent visions and conflicting perspectives among partners can stall business progress.

• The requirement for separate tax returns can be seen as an administrative burden.

• Profit-sharing means dividing earnings with partners, potentially impacting individual income.

Limited Partnerships

In contrast to our earlier chapters, Limited Partnerships (LPs) require a deliberate and formal selection process, involving registration with your state authorities.

Within the structure of Limited Partnerships, two distinct partner roles emerge: the General Partner and the Limited Partner. The General Partner shoulders the managerial responsibilities and carries personal liability for the company's day-to-day operations, while Limited Partners take on a more hands-off, passive role, primarily contributing as investors in the business.

While LPs do share certain similarities with general partnerships, they present a unique advantage - Limited Partners typically enjoy protection from personal liability in the event of company-related damages, rendering LPs particularly appealing to those seeking a passive investment role. Nevertheless, it's crucial to acknowledge that assuming the position of General Partner in an LP exposes you to personal liability for the company's obligations, alongside the associated management costs.

Pros:

• Clear distinction between General Partners and Limited Partners.

• Managerial flexibility for General Partners.

• Passive investment opportunity for Limited Partners.

• Limited liability protection for Limited Partners.

• Attractive to passive investors seeking reduced liability.

• Potential tax benefits similar to other partnerships.

Cons:

• General Partners assume personal liability for company obligations.

• Additional management costs when a General Partner is involved.

• Requires formal registration and documentation.

• Potential for internal disputes due to differing visions.

• Limited access to capital compared to corporations.

• General Partners may lack specialized expertise or resources.

C Corporations

Now turn our attention to the C Corporation. The C Corporation is regarded as one of the most advanced business entities due to its complete separation from individuals, both legally and in terms of taxation.

While most business entities are categorized as pass-through entities, meaning they are linked to individuals and subject to individual tax rates, the C Corporation stands apart with its unique tax separation. For instance, consider a scenario where you, as a single filer, have $200,000 in business profits. In a pass-through entity, these profits are taxed at the individual rate, which can be as high as 32 percent. However, C Corporation profits are subject to a specific flat tax rate, which, for 2022, stands at 21 percent. This significant tax difference underscores the appeal of C Corporations.

It's important to note that many of the largest companies in America are structured as C Corporations.

Pros:

• Limited Liability Protection: Shareholders aren't personally liable for company debts.

• Favorable Taxation: Flat corporate tax rates can be more advantageous.

• Tax Deductions: Eligible for various tax deductions, including charitable donations.

• Fundraising Ease: The ability to issue stock options and shares simplifies fundraising.

• Credibility: Conveys stability and trustworthiness.

• Scalability: Well-suited for growth and expansion.

Cons:

• Administrative Complexity: More paperwork and requirements.

• Tax Complexity: Requires tax planning and professional assistance.

• Higher Costs: Additional expenses, including compliance costs.

• Double Taxation: Profits may face double taxation when distributed to shareholders.

• Government Compliance: Must meet regulatory requirements, like shareholder meetings and bylaws.

S Corporation

While some may engage in debates regarding whether an S corporation qualifies as a distinct business entity or is merely a tax election, the reality remains consistent. Regardless of your stance on this matter, it's imperative to understand the functioning of an S corp.

An S corporation essentially embodies a fusion of attributes from both C corporations and other business structures. It extends the invaluable benefit of limited liability protection, safeguarding your assets from the business's financial obligations. Moreover, an S corporation retains the capacity to issue stocks, facilitating the process of capital generation for your company. However, what sets it apart is its taxation framework. Instead of being subjected to a fixed corporate tax rate, an S corporation assumes the role of a pass-through entity.

This tax classification introduces a high degree of flexibility into its business structure, rendering it an enticing choice for prospective owners or shareholders. The key advantages of being associated with an S corporation encompass personal liability protection, exemption from double taxation or corporate tax obligations, and the absence of self-employment taxes applied to owner distributions.

Nonetheless, it's vital to acknowledge the attendant drawbacks. Operating under the banner of an S corporation necessitates the disbursement of a reasonable salary to oneself, adhering to tax regulations. Furthermore, while the issuance of stock is a viable option, there exist limitations on the extent to which stock can be allocated. Additionally, compliance with governmental prerequisites, such as the formulation of bylaws and the conduct of meetings, remains an essential responsibility.

In my perspective, S corporations rank as the second most potent business entities, trailing closely behind C corporations. However, this does not imply that the hasty establishment of an S corporation or a C corporation is advisable. Your choice should be contingent upon your business's specific stage and requirements, as these entities may entail associated costs. It's also worth noting that the realm of non-profit corporations constitutes an entirely separate category, which we shall leave unexplored for now.

Pros:

• Personal Liability Protection: Shields personal assets from business liabilities.

• Tax Flexibility: Taxed as a pass-through entity, avoiding corporate tax rates.

• No Self-Employment Taxes: No self-employment taxes on owner distributions.

• Stock Issuance: The ability to issue stock simplifies capital generation.

• Enhanced Credibility: S Corporations convey stability and trustworthiness.

Cons:

• Required Reasonable Salary: Owners must pay themselves a reasonable salary, following tax regulations.

• Stock Issuance Limits: Restrictions on the amount of stock that can be allocated.

• Government Requirements: Must comply with governmental prerequisites, including creating bylaws and holding meetings.

LLC

Now, let's delve into the sixth business entity on our list, one that you're likely familiar with the Limited Liability Company, commonly known as the LLC. If you've conducted any research into launching a business, you've probably encountered numerous recommendations suggesting the establishment of an LLC, and rightfully so. In my assessment, LLCs epitomize the pinnacle of business entity flexibility.

As you've traversed through this list, you've undoubtedly noticed the array of advantages and disadvantages associated with each entity type. However, an LLC can be likened to a harmonious blend of the most advantageous attributes. Here's why:

First and foremost, an LLC extends the priceless benefit of limited liability protection, shielding your assets from potential business-related obligations. Moreover, it provides you with the latitude to select the preferred tax classification for your business, whether opting for taxation as a corporation or as a pass-through entity. Remarkably, an LLC imposes fewer government-imposed prerequisites compared to other entities.

The inherent drawbacks of an LLC are notably scarce. One of the few considerations entails the obligation to formally register your business with the Secretary of State and meet the accompanying annual fee requirements.

In essence, the Limited Liability Company emerges as the quintessential choice for those seeking a business entity that combines the finest attributes, encompassing personal asset protection, tax flexibility, and minimal regulatory burdens.

Pros:

• Personal Liability Protection: Safeguards personal assets from business liabilities.

• Tax Flexibility: Allows businesses to choose their tax classification, whether as a corporation or a pass-through entity.

• Fewer Government Requirements: Involves fewer regulatory requirements compared to other business structures.

• Simplified Management: Less formalities and paperwork in day-to-day operations.

• Enhanced Credibility: Can convey professionalism and trustworthiness to clients and partners.

• Scalability: Suited for businesses aiming for growth and expansion.

Cons:

• Registration and Annual Fees: Requires registration with the secretary of state and payment of annual fees.

How to Select the Optimal Business Structure

When it comes to selecting the optimal business entity for your needs, there are two crucial points I'd like to emphasize. Firstly, you are the one who comprehends your business's vision and operational strategy better than anyone else. Thus, I strongly encourage you to conduct thorough research and meticulously weigh the advantages and disadvantages associated with each business entity.

Secondly, I will delineate my list and tiers, which serve as a helpful framework for individuals seeking guidance in making their own informed decisions regarding the most fitting entity structure.

Tier Number One - Sole Proprietorships and General Partnerships: This tier is an excellent choice for individuals who prioritize swift initiation, minimal paperwork, and do not anticipate earning more than $250,000 in income. Sole proprietors and independent contractors working under larger companies may benefit from added liability protections offered by their employers, coupled with necessary insurance policies.

Tier Number Two - Limited Liability Companies (LLCs) and Partnerships: Entrepreneurs venturing independently can find great value in this tier. It provides limited liability protection while offering scalability. As income grows, you can opt for corporate taxation. It is also an ideal starting point for establishing business credit and securing initial capital for future projects.

Tier Number Three - S-Corporations (S-Corps): Once your business gains momentum, an S-Corp might be the right choice. It accommodates high-demand products or services, enabling the issuance of stocks to raise capital. Additionally, S-Corps allows business owners to put themselves on payroll, reducing self-employment taxes. These entities are well-suited for growing companies in need of extra capital or seeking tax advantages.

Tier Number Four - C-Corporations (C-Corps): Reserved for businesses projecting substantial revenue or aiming to raise significant capital from investors or shareholders, C-Corps are perfect. They require an appetite for aggressive reinvestment while maintaining a positive growth trajectory.

In essence, many individuals might initially find Tier Two most suitable, allowing them to grow and evolve as their business prospers. The tier system provides a structured approach to choosing the business structure that aligns best with your specific goals and circumstances.

Who Should Establish Your Business Entity?

Sometimes, I receive inquiries about the best approach for setting up a business entity. People often contemplate whether they should do it themselves, engage a tax attorney, or enlist the services of an accountant. These three options are the most common, so let's delve into the distinctions among them.

First and foremost, consider your knowledge and expertise in this matter. Now, let's briefly discuss the primary differences between a tax accountant and a tax attorney.

Tax Accountant: When consulting a tax accountant to establish your business entity, they will predominantly focus on the tax and financial implications of your chosen structure. They may inquire about factors like your initial investment, projected revenue, the number of partners or investors, and the operational structure. This information enables them to comprehensively assess how your entity selection will influence your tax obligations.

Tax Attorney: Conversely, tax attorneys are primarily concerned with the legal ramifications associated with different business entities. They will ask questions about your assets, asset protection strategies, potential asset transfers, and any legal risks inherent to your business. This in-depth analysis helps them determine how your choice of entity may impact you and your assets from a legal perspective.

It's important to note that while both parties possess knowledge of tax and legal matters, they each specialize in their respective areas of expertise.

Chapter 6: Business Registration and Employer Identification Number (EIN)

The process of registering your business may vary from state to state, but here are some common requirements to consider:

1. Business Name: You'll need to provide the name of your business.

2. Filer Information: Include the name and address of the person filing or registering the business.

3. Principal Office Address: Specify the mailing address of the principal office for the business, which can be a home office.

4. Registered Agent: Provide the name and address of the registered agent. The registered agent is responsible for receiving official correspondence on behalf of the business.

5. Partners' Information: Share the names and addresses of all partners involved in the business.

6. Operations Agreement: Depending on your state's requirements, you may need an operations agreement. This document outlines the rights and responsibilities of each LLC member and includes details on profit distribution, decision-making processes, admitting new members, and handling successorship.

7. Payment: Be prepared to submit the required payment for the registration process.

Registering your business typically involves providing basic information such as names and addresses. You can initiate this process by visiting your state's Secretary of State office website. Conduct a business name search to ensure your desired name is available in your state. Then, follow the provided instructions and prompts to complete the registration.

Two common challenges that new business owners face during registration are appointing a registered agent and creating an operations agreement. Here's some guidance on these aspects:

Registered Agent: A registered agent is the person who receives official correspondence, notices, and legal documents on behalf of the business. While some entrepreneurs believe they need an attorney to serve as their registered agent, it's not always required. Many business owners, including myself, act as registered agents for their businesses.

Operations Agreement: Even if your state doesn't mandate it, having a well-structured operations agreement is advisable, especially if you have business partners. This legal document outlines the rights and responsibilities of each LLC member and covers various aspects, such as profit distribution, decision-making procedures, admitting new members, and handling changes in ownership. You don't necessarily need to hire an attorney to draft an operations agreement. Online templates, like those available through Law Depot, can help you create a professional operations agreement tailored to your business needs. Simply select your state and follow the step-by-step guidance to create your agreement.

Once you've completed your operations agreement and made the necessary payment to your Secretary of State, typically within a few weeks, you will receive your articles of incorporation. This signifies that your business is officially registered and ready to progress to the next step.

Employer Identification Number (EIN)

So, what exactly is an EIN?

In simple terms, an EIN functions as a Social Security number for your business. The acronym EIN stands for Employer Identification Number, and as the name implies, it's a unique number issued by the IRS to distinguish one business from another. You may also encounter the term FEIN, which includes the word "federal," or it might be referred to as your business's Tax Identification Number.

Why do you need an EIN?

The key term to remember here is "employer." If your business employs or plans to employ individuals, you'll require an EIN. Moreover, both partnerships and multi-member LLCs are obligated to obtain an EIN. This is because these business structures must file a partnership return with the IRS, and this necessitates the use of an EIN.

While technically, sole proprietorships or single-member LLCs without employees can function without an EIN, there are compelling reasons to consider obtaining one:

1. Many banks require an EIN to open a business bank account. Separating your business finances from personal finances is crucial for accurate expense tracking, building business credit, and qualifying for loans.

2. If you have plans to hire employees in the future, having an EIN in advance ensures you are prepared.

3. An EIN can enhance your business's credibility. Working with other businesses often carries more appeal than dealing solely with individual entrepreneurs.

4. Maintaining an EIN helps establish a clear boundary between your assets and those belonging to the business.

Knowing why you might want an EIN is valuable, but it's equally important to understand how to obtain one.

How to apply for an EIN:

Thankfully, applying for an EIN is both straightforward and free. The process can be completed through the IRS website, typically within five minutes. Note that you can use the IRS portal between 7:00 a.m. and 10:00 p.m. Eastern Standard Time.

Here's how it works:

1. The IRS will ask you to specify your business's legal structure. You can choose from six options on the first page, with the option to explore 23 other legal entity types. For this explanation, we'll walk you through the process of obtaining an EIN for an LLC.

2. You will provide basic details about your LLC, such as the state where it's located and the number of members it will have. Your answers will determine the subsequent screens you encounter.

3. Depending on whether you specify one or more members, you will face different confirmation screens. This is because single-member LLCs are taxed differently from multi-member LLCs in the eyes of the IRS.

4. You'll be prompted to select your business's purpose for obtaining an EIN, choosing from five options. Most people will choose either "for hiring employees" or "for banking purposes."

5. The next question involves identifying the responsible party applying for the EIN, which can be the owner, a member, a manager, or a third-party designee. If you're applying on someone else's behalf, additional information will be required.

6. Afterward, you'll provide your company's physical and mailing addresses.

7. You'll then be asked to share various details about your LLC, including its legal name, trade names or DBAs, physical location, state of formation, and the month and year of formation.

8. You'll encounter screens with specific questions, such as whether your business uses trucks over 55,000 pounds, is involved in gambling, needs to file quarterly Federal Excise Tax Returns (Form 720), or produces/sells alcohol, tobacco, or firearms. The critical

question here is whether you anticipate having employees for whom you'll need W-2s in the next year.

9. Finally, you'll fill out screens regarding your business's intended use and confirm the accuracy of the information provided.

Although this process may seem daunting, rest assured that it can typically be completed swiftly—often in under five minutes. The IRS has streamlined the application, ensuring a smooth experience for applicants.

Establishing Your Business Bank Accounts

One common error that novice entrepreneurs often commit during their initial stages is commingling business finances with their personal finances. This can lead to complications, as it becomes easy to lose track of the distinction between your business's financial performance and your personal tax obligations.

It's crucial to maintain accurate records of your income and expenditures to facilitate smooth reporting to the IRS during tax season. When you utilize business bank accounts with digital transaction capabilities, it becomes significantly more convenient to monitor all your financial activities. I strongly recommend setting up these accounts soon after obtaining your articles of incorporation and EIN.

Chapter 7: Create Your MVP Strategy

What is an MVP

The concept of MVP, or "minimum viable product," holds a significant role in the world of business and innovation. It represents the most streamlined version of a product that a company can put out into the market. The primary aim of an MVP is to attract those initial customers and elicit invaluable feedback from them. In essence, it functions as a practical form of market research.

In the dynamic world of entrepreneurship, a Minimum Viable Product (MVP) is your compass for navigating the early stages of your business venture. However, it's crucial to approach your MVP with the right mindset, a mindset that avoids the common pitfalls many budding entrepreneurs stumble into.

Assembling Your MVP: A Strategic Shift

A common misconception among entrepreneurs is the belief that starting a business requires an arduous journey of product development, spanning months or even years. You pour your heart and soul into creating a product and then unleash it onto the market, hoping that customers will flock to your offering.

The key to avoiding this common pitfall is to shift your approach, and it begins by crafting a Minimum Viable Product with a laser focus on lead generation.

Why Lead Generation is Paramount

In the world of business, there's a golden rule: "Everything is Downstream of Lead Generation." If you can't generate leads for your business, you won't be able to generate sales – plain and simple. A lead, in essence, is any indicator of interest from potential customers.

The objective of your MVP is crystal clear: Generate those leads. To do this, you must offer something of value for free and observe if people express interest. Charging for your MVP at this stage is not advisable because if you can't attract people with a free offering, getting them to pay is an uphill battle.

Two MVP Options for Lead Generation

Here are two MVP strategies that you can implement for free, tailored to your specific business domain:

The Free Webinar: Crafting captivating content and adopting effective presentation techniques are crucial elements of this phase. Don't forget to map out your promotional strategy well in advance—building anticipation and attracting potential  customers are key to your webinar's success.

Once your webinar takes shape, it's time for a pivotal stage—testing your MVP with potential customers. Feedback is your most precious asset during this phase, and we'll use a variety of methods like surveys, user testing sessions, and focus groups to gather invaluable insights. This feedback will serve as the guiding star, illuminating the path to refining your MVP and polishing your value proposition to resonate deeply with your audience.

These instruments can streamline your efforts and enhance your success. Standout options include:

• Luma: A versatile platform that provides the stage for your webinar's performance.

• Zoom: A trusted and feature-rich choice for hosting webinars that captivate your audience.

• Google Meet: Google's robust offering, equipped with webinar capabilities to engage your audience effectively.

Suppose you're launching a fitness coaching business. Rather than diving headfirst into product development, you can create a free webinar, such as "Unlocking Your Fitness Potential." This live, online event provides valuable insights into fitness trends, nutrition, and customized workout routines. Because it's free, it attracts sign-ups and generates those coveted leads.

2. The Interactive Scorecard (Quiz Online): Imagine you're venturing into financial services. Instead of pushing your financial offerings immediately, you could design an online scorecard, much like a quiz, to gauge users' financial preferences and needs. This interactive approach is engaging, and people love participating in online quizzes. Plus, it offers a wealth of data to validate your business idea.

Creating Your MVP Scorecard

Let's take a closer look at the Scorecard MVP strategy, which I've recently integrated into my own entrepreneurial endeavors. It's essentially a sophisticated online quiz, and here's how you can create one:

• Use a dedicated app like Score App, which streamlines the process. It's incredibly user-friendly, and you can find a link in the template for a free 30-day trial.

• Define your primary goal for the scorecard. In our example, it's lead generation.

• Craft engaging questions that align with your business and gather valuable data about user preferences.

• Determine the possible outcomes of the scorecard. For a custom wand business, it could be matching users with different wand types like Dragon Heartstring, Phoenix Feather, or Unicorn Hair.

• Set up your scorecard, ensuring it's attractive and user-friendly.

• Once users complete the scorecard, you'll have their contact details. Prompt them to engage further, perhaps with a free consultation or discussion about your offerings.

By adopting the Scorecard MVP approach, you can swiftly generate leads, validate your business concept, and collect invaluable data for future refinement. This versatile strategy empowers entrepreneurs to stay agile and responsive in an ever-evolving business landscape. Remember, the key is to start with lead generation, as everything else flows downstream from there.

Why you shouldn't avoid the MVP creation

Considering the creation of a Minimum Viable Product (MVP) can be a game-changer for entrepreneurs, offering them a strategic advantage in the world of business. Here are some compelling reasons why you should contemplate developing an MVP:

1. Swift Validation: An MVP allows you to promptly test your business idea and assumptions. This rapid validation helps you determine whether your concept holds promise.

2. Early Problem Detection: By releasing an MVP, you can uncover potential issues at the initial stages of development. This proactive approach enables you to address problems before they become significant roadblocks.

3. Customer Insights: Launching an MVP provides invaluable insights into your target audience's needs and preferences. This firsthand knowledge empowers you to tailor your product to meet customer expectations effectively.

4. Time and Cost Savings: Developing a full-scale, feature-rich product can be time-consuming and expensive. An MVP minimizes these costs by focusing on core functionality, ensuring you don't sink resources into unnecessary features.

5. Risk Mitigation: Launching an MVP reduces the risk of making substantial investments in a product that may not resonate with your audience. It's a prudent approach to testing the waters before diving in.

6. Client-Sourced Ideas: Gathering feedback from potential clients through your MVP can provide you with invaluable ideas for refining and enhancing your product. Their input becomes a roadmap for future MVP development.

7. Enhanced Product Quality: The iterative nature of MVP development allows you to gradually build a superior, more polished product based on user feedback and real-world testing.

Now, consider the cost of not releasing an MVP. Picture this scenario: You invest several years and substantial resources into developing a web application. Your team includes developers, graphic designers, and marketing specialists. You continuously refine the product, adding more features and seeking innovation. However, when you finally launch it, you discover that users are uninterested because the fundamental features don't align with their needs. This results in wasted time and money.

Choosing an MVP approach, on the other hand, safeguards you from such setbacks. It enables you to launch a product that gauges user interest and identifies areas for improvement. By taking incremental steps, you significantly reduce the stress and costs associated with an ill-fated product launch. An MVP is your insurance policy against professional setbacks and financial losses.

Other types and examples of MVP

1. Concierge MVP - Delivering Personalized Experiences: In the realm of business, think of Concierge MVP as akin to offering tailored assistance to customers to determine their precise needs. A compelling example is Manuel Rosso, the visionary founder of Food on the Table. In the early days, he didn't possess a website or a concrete product to sell. Instead, he provided personalized services by crafting custom recipes and grocery lists during in-store visits, all for a nominal monthly fee of $10. This narrative epitomizes the Concierge MVP approach, which has proven to be highly successful in delivering tailored business solutions.

3. Landing Page MVP - Testing Market Waters: A landing page serves as a strategic tool. It acts as a digital storefront, offering a specific product or service, detailed descriptions, usage demonstrations, and a prominent Call to Action button, encouraging users to take action, such as subscribing to a mailing list. By deploying a landing page, you can conduct invaluable market research, assess interest in your offering, and collect valuable contact information from potential clients. Just as in the business world, where market research informs product launches, this MVP approach helps you navigate the competitive landscape with precision.

4. Email MVP - Engaging Your Audience: If you already possess a customer base in the business sphere and are contemplating the introduction of a new product or service, the Email MVP strategy comes into play. It entails sending targeted emails to gauge the interest of your existing customer base. A positive response acts as a green light, signaling that your product or service idea resonates with your audience, thereby paving the way for further development and refinement.

Here are some examples of Minimum Viable Products (MVPs) across various industries:

1. Dropbox: Dropbox started as a simple MVP. Its founder, Drew Houston, created a basic file-sharing service with a video demonstrating how it worked. This video served as a call to action to sign up for early access. It allowed them to gauge interest and validate the concept before investing heavily in development.

2. Buffer: Buffer, a social media management platform, began with a minimal version that allowed users to schedule tweets. It was a simple tool with limited features, but it addressed a specific pain point for social media managers. Over time, Buffer expanded and added more features based on user feedback.

3. Zappos: Zappos, the online shoe retailer, started by taking pictures of shoes from local stores and posting them online. When customers place orders, they would purchase the shoes from the local store and ship them. This proved the demand for an online shoe store before they invested in building their inventory.

4. Craigslist: Craigslist is a classic example of an MVP. It started as a basic email list for local events and classified ads. Over time, it added more features and categories based on user needs, becoming a global online marketplace.

5. Airbnb: Airbnb's MVP was a simple website offering air mattresses and breakfast for attendees of a design conference in San Francisco. This allowed the founders to test the concept of renting out extra space in their home. The positive response from early users validated the idea, and Airbnb has since grown into a global hospitality platform.

6. Instagram: Instagram's MVP was a photo-sharing app with a few filters and basic social features. It focused on the core value of sharing photos quickly and easily. As it gained traction, Instagram added more features and evolved into a major social media platform.

7. Uber: Uber's initial MVP was a black car service app in San Francisco. It allowed users to request rides, and drivers to use their vehicles. The MVP served a specific market and proved the demand for convenient transportation services. Uber then expanded to include various ride types and geographic areas.

An example of MVP used by Anthony the plumber to acquire more customers

Anthony started by setting up a Facebook page showcasing his plumbing services. He began posting photos and videos of his work, highlighting his expertise, attention to detail, and commitment to customer satisfaction. These posts showcased everything from fixing leaky faucets to tackling complex pipe installations.

To his delight, people began to take notice. His friends and satisfied customers liked and commented on his posts, praising his skills and professionalism. Anthony's MVP was starting to gain traction.

In these online interactions, Anthony learned what customers were looking for in a plumber, he understood their concerns, preferences, and pain points.

With each successful job, Anthony's reputation grew. Happy customers left glowing reviews on his Facebook page, further bolstering his credibility.

Customers found it easy to contact him through the platform, whether it was to inquire about services, request a quote, or schedule an appointment.

Anthony's MVP had evolved into a thriving digital presence that not only showcased his work but also facilitated meaningful interactions with customers.

Chapter 8: Develop the Product or Service and launch it

Developing

$\mathcal{N}$ow that you have a clear understanding of your offer and the primary value you aim to provide, it's time to create your product or service around that proposition. Thanks to the insights garnered through our Minimum Viable Product (MVP) approach, our product or service can be meticulously tailored to precisely match the market's demands. The data-driven decisions made during the MVP phase have allowed us to optimize every aspect of our offering, resulting in a solution that is perfectly aligned with the market's requirements.

Let's consider a few examples to illustrate this concept:

1. Value Proposition: Speed

• Suppose one of your core value propositions is speed, intending to outperform competitors in your niche. In this case, you would optimize your product or service for speed, ensuring that it delivers on this promise. This could involve streamlining processes, using efficient technologies, or implementing rapid response mechanisms to meet customer needs quickly.

2. Value Proposition: Innovation

• If your objective is to offer something unique that sets your business apart, innovation becomes crucial. Focus on developing new and creative solutions that differentiate your product or service from existing offerings. This may require extensive research, brainstorming, and a commitment to staying at the forefront of your industry's advancements.

Addressing Self-Limiting Beliefs:

It's common to grapple with self-limiting beliefs, such as doubting your company's trustworthiness due to a lack of experience or expertise. However, it's essential to recognize that business success is rooted in problem-solving. Here's a perspective to keep in mind:

1. Solving Real Market Problems:

• Business success hinges on your ability to address genuine market needs and challenges. If you can effectively resolve these issues, your business will gain credibility and earn the trust of customers. So, focus on your problem-solving skills and your commitment to making a positive impact.

2. Confidence and Research:

• Confidence in your ability to research, adapt, and learn is invaluable. With determination and a willingness to acquire knowledge, you can quickly become an expert in your field. Don't let external judgments deter you; instead, channel that energy into continuous self-improvement.

10 best marketing channels you can use to launch your product or service

Numerous marketing avenues are available for your small business to explore. We aim to simplify the array of marketing options at your disposal to ensure the success of your campaign.

As stated by Peter Drucker, who is frequently credited as the father of contemporary management: "There are only two things in a firm that earn money: innovation and marketing. Everything else is cost."

Yet, in this plethora of marketing channels, the question arises: how do you discern the best fit for your needs?

Within this chapter, we delve into ten marketing distribution channels and elucidate how to wield them effectively in your favor.

Quick Overview: Optimal Marketing Channels for Your Business

1. Search Engine Optimization (SEO)

2. Content Marketing

3. Email Marketing

4. Social Media Marketing

5. Word of Mouth Marketing (WOMM)

6. Influencer Marketing

7. Offline Advertising

8. Online Advertising

9. Partnership Marketing

10. Community Building

The Ideal Marketing Channels for Your Small Business

Regardless of your business's size, there exists an extensive array of marketing channels at your disposal. However, the crucial inquiry is: do these align with your objectives and requirements?

To help you navigate this terrain, here is an exploration of the ten most prevalent marketing channels that contemporary businesses employ:

1. Search Engine Optimization (SEO) According to HubSpot, 62% of consumers utilize search engines to gather information about new businesses, products, or services, with 41% relying on search engines for their purchasing decisions. Given the sheer volume of Google searches conducted annually, search engines remain the primary method for online information retrieval.

SEO involves the process of enhancing your website's visibility in search engine results pages (SERPs) for specific keywords or terms. This strategy facilitates easy access to your content for those seeking information related to your niche. The advantage of SEO is that it generates "organic" website traffic without the need for paid ad placement.

While SEO continually evolves, some fundamental principles remain constant, such as crawlability, site structure, keywords, and backlinks.

SEO Tips:

• Aim for first-page search engine rankings because 75% of internet visitors hardly ever scroll past the first SERP page.

• Utilize tools like Google Search Console, Ahrefs Keywords Explorer, and Google Keyword Planner to master keyword optimization.

• Continue to produce engaging content to draw visitors and gain recognition from search engines.

• To suit the rising popularity of mobile device usage, optimize your website for mobile search.

2. Content marketing constantly hitting potential and current customers with "buy" messages might turn them off and harm your brand's reputation. To engage a particular market segment, content marketing focuses on regularly creating and distributing valuable

information, such as blog posts, videos, infographics, eBooks, case studies, and interviews.

Content marketing aims to achieve various objectives, including brand building, lead generation, customer retention, increased sales, pre-and post-sale information dissemination, support for SEO and social media efforts, and establishing authority and reputation.

Content Marketing Tips:

• Understand that content marketing is a long-term endeavor, requiring consistent delivery of valuable content to build trust and authority.

• Integrate content marketing into your overall small business marketing plan, combining it with other digital marketing channels.

3. Email marketing is a powerful way to connect with people interested in your business, product, website, or brand because there are more than 4.3 billion email subscribers globally. This channel promotes connections with present and potential customers and is frequently used for brand development, information sharing, and the delivery of targeted marketing messages.

Email Marketing Tips:

• Build your email list through consent, avoiding purchased lists from dubious sources.

• Personalize your campaigns to enhance relevance and minimize unsubscribe rates.

4. Social Media Marketing Social media usage is widespread, with approximately 3.5 billion users worldwide. Platforms like Twitter, LinkedIn, Snapchat, Instagram, Facebook, YouTube, and Pinterest enable brand building, audience growth, relationship building, and sales generation.

Social media marketing is versatile and can encompass a wide range of strategies, including organic posting, paid advertising, influencer partnerships, and community engagement.

Social Media Marketing Tips:

• Integrate social media with other digital marketing strategies for maximum impact.

• Understand your audience thoroughly to craft tailored content.

• Maintain consistency through a social media calendar.

5. According to the study on Word of Mouth Marketing (WOMM), 83% of Americans are more inclined to buy a good or service if a friend or family member recommends it. When customers communicate their satisfaction with a good or service, whether naturally or as a result of deliberate marketing efforts, this is known as WOMM.

WOMM Tips:

• Encourage customers to create and share user-generated content.

• Leverage hashtags for spreading promotional campaigns on social media.

• Display user reviews prominently on your website.

6. Using influencers: influencer marketing makes use of people who have devoted social media audiences to mention or recommend your product or service to their followers. Product reviews, sponsored content, team ups, freebies, or platform takeovers are some examples of this.

Influencer Marketing Tips:

• Focus on engagement rates rather than follower counts.

• Choose influencers aligned with your brand values.

• Allow influencers creative freedom in content creation.

7. Offline Advertising Despite the digital age, offline advertising remains a viable channel for reaching individuals who don't rely on the internet for information. Methods include business cards, local event giveaways, speaking engagements, trade magazines, print advertising, direct mail, and more.

Offline Advertising Tips:

• Combine offline advertising with online conversion activities.

• Ensure consistent branding across all channels.

8. Internet Marketing: utilizing the internet to market goods, services, or marketing messages is known as online advertising. It includes display advertising, affiliate marketing, sponsored social, native advertising, remarketing, and video ads, among other things.

Online Advertising Tips:

• Select relevant keywords for PPC campaigns.

• Precisely target your desired audience.

9. Partnership Marketing: collaboration between two brands is required for partnership marketing to produce profitable campaigns. By collaborating with businesses that provide complementary goods

or services, this economical method increases market penetration and improves brand recognition.

Partnership Marketing Tips:

• Choose reputable brands aligned with your goals.

• Establish clear goals and metrics for tracking performance.

• Implement robust reporting systems to track partnership-generated leads or sales.

10. Community Building Building a brand community around your business can be a highly effective marketing strategy. Companies like Harley-Davidson, Apple, and Lego have successfully leveraged brand communities for benefits like brand loyalty, authenticity, feedback, user-generated content, and marketing efficiency.

Brand communities often take the form of online forums, social media groups, or physical events where customers and fans can interact and share their experiences.

Community Building Tips:

• Building a community takes time, effort, and patience to cultivate lasting connections.

• Actively engage with community members and prioritize relationships over constant self-promotion.

While an array of marketing channels exists, success doesn't necessitate adopting every available option. Instead, evaluate the channels aligned with your goals, continually refine your strategy based on results, and prioritize those that yield the highest return on investment.

If you want to be the best, learn from the best

Let us take as an example how Apple, an iconic tech giant, has mastered the art of product launches, with record-breaking sales and global anticipation. While Apple's massive brand presence plays a significant role in its success, there are strategic principles that any business can apply to orchestrate a successful product launch.

Humanize Your Product: Steve Jobs, the face of Apple, rarely delved into the technical intricacies of their products during launches. Instead, he artfully connected with the audience by highlighting how Apple's innovations would simplify and enhance their lives. The key takeaway here is to focus on how your product addresses real-life problems and improves the daily experiences of your target audience.

Engage Key Influencers Early: Apple strategically collaborates with bloggers and thought leaders well in advance of their product launches. These influencers ignite conversations and anticipation even before a product is officially unveiled. While you may not possess Apple's global reach, you can engage with the media and influencers within your industry ahead of your launch. Building these relationships can lead to valuable coverage and recognition.

Champion Innovation: Apple stands out for its revolutionary products that redefine entire industries. Regardless of your company's size, you have the potential to be a catalyst for change. Dare to challenge the status quo, embrace innovative ideas, and envision a future that resonates with your customers. By doing so, you can inspire others and differentiate your brand in the market.

Elevate Your Launch into an Event: Apple transforms product launches into grand spectacles, temporarily closing their online store to signify the significance of the event. At the heart of these presentations is the CEO, who assumes the role of a captivating showman. While you may not have Apple's budget, creating an unforgettable product launch event or a compelling online experience can significantly enhance your product's visibility and impact.

Harness Pre-Orders: Apple consistently offers pre-orders for their new products, generating substantial sales momentum before the official launch. Even if your business is not at Apple's scale, you can still leverage this strategy. Allow your most dedicated customers to pre-order your product, driving initial sales and excitement. If pre-orders are not feasible, establish a mechanism for interested buyers to sign up for updates, ensuring they are the first to know when the product becomes available.

Prioritize Aesthetics and Shareability: Apple recognizes the importance of product aesthetics. Their commitment to elegant design ensures that customers not only find their products functional but also visually appealing. An attractive design motivates customers to proudly share their purchases, leading to increased brand visibility and sales. Remember, aesthetics matter, both online and offline.

Sustain Suspense and Curiosity: Apple's product details are often shrouded in secrecy until the launch date, sparking immense curiosity and speculation. You can adopt a similar strategy by deliberately releasing limited information about your upcoming product. This element of mystery can create a sense of anticipation and excitement among your target audience.

In conclusion, you do not need Apple's vast resources to execute a successful product launch. What you require is a well-thought-out plan, control over the flow of information, collaboration with key influencers, and a sharp focus on how your product improves the lives of your customers. With the right strategy, your product launch can generate significant buzz, even if you're a small or emerging business."

Chapter 9: Going Beyond Success

Product-Market Fit, Business Expansion, and Innovation

*T*here comes a time when your company hits its stride, customers love what you're doing, and things are going great. But here's the thing: success isn't a one-time thing; it's a continuous journey. In today's fast-changing world, you've got to keep your product-market fit sharp, expand your business wisely, and add cool new stuff to stand out from the competition. How? Well, by paying attention to your customers, keeping an eye on what the competition is up to, and staying in tune with the market you're in, whether it's in your city, country, online, or globally.

The Ever-Changing Market

Just when you think you've figured it all out, the market shifts. People's tastes change, new technologies emerge, and competitors are always cooking up something new. What worked yesterday might not work tomorrow. So, getting your product-market fit right isn't a "one-and-done" thing – it's an ongoing process.

Listen to Your Customers

Your customers are like your North Star. They guide you to success, and they'll keep you there if you pay attention. Keep collecting feedback from them. Chat with them through surveys, online forums, or wherever they hang out. Learn about their pain points, dreams, and what they expect from you.

Use their feedback to make your product or service even better. This isn't just about keeping your current customers happy – it's also about attracting new ones by adapting to their changing needs.

Keep an Eye on the Competition

As you grow, the competition gets fiercer. You've got to stay sharp. Watch what your competitors are up to – their strategies, what they're selling, and how they treat their customers. Find those gaps in the market that they might be missing. Stand out by offering something special or fixing problems others haven't.

And don't just look at local rivals. Sometimes, your competition comes from across the globe. Know what's happening in your industry, no matter where it's happening.

Fit Your Market, Wherever It Is

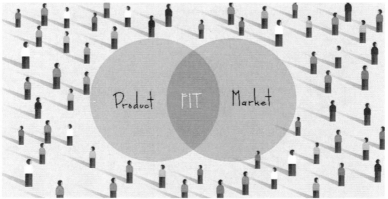

If you're thinking about growing your business, you've got to be adaptable. Whether you're thinking local, national, or global, understand the different needs and tastes of each market.

Do your homework – study the local culture, economics, and rules in each area you want to expand to. Make sure your product or service clicks with the locals while keeping your brand identity strong. Going global might mean changing your marketing, distribution, and pricing strategies.

Innovation Is the Name of the Game

When you're scaling up, think about creating new things. Adding fresh products or services doesn't just keep your customers interested – it can set you apart from the competition. Make innovation part of your company's DNA. Encourage everyone to think up new ideas and give them a shot.

Innovation isn't just about throwing new stuff out there; it's about making your existing offerings better and different. Use new technologies and trends to stay ahead of the game. Creating new things keeps your audience excited and can bring in new customers too.

The Significance of Tools for Entrepreneurs

One of the most crucial entrepreneur tips is to embrace the use of tools. In today's business landscape, productivity and collaboration are paramount. If you want to enhance your team's efficiency, remember that tools are indispensable. There's no need to reinvent the wheel when it's already been invented. Instead of relying on pen and paper for manual tasks, consider the plethora of online tools available.

These tools facilitate clear communication among team members, task prioritization, delegation of responsibilities, planning, performance measurement, and more. Embrace innovation and be open to trying new tools; they not only save you time and money but also reduce the risk of errors. As an entrepreneur, your time is valuable, so automate repetitive tasks whenever possible. Strive for efficiency!

Chapter 10: Accounting

Recognizing the potentially dry nature of accounting, it's important to acknowledge that delving into numbers may not always be the most thrilling endeavor, especially when your primary focus is steering your business towards success. Nevertheless, empirical research indicates a rather disconcerting reality: 9 out of 10 businesses face failure due to their inability to comprehend their financial intricacies.

The undeniable veracity here is that a profound comprehension of accounting translates directly into an intimate understanding of your business. In this chapter we will systematically dissect the subject of accounting.

The topic of accounting is very broad and important and a single chapter is not enough to delve into every facet of it, we'll write a book specifically dedicated to this topic, in any case it is essential that you know the basics as you are about to embark on your entrepreneurship journey.

What is Accounting?

Accounting is a systematic procedure encompassing the recording, organization, comprehension, reporting, and analysis of financial data. While this may initially seem intricate, it can be dissected into three fundamental components:

Recording All Transactions: The initial facet involves meticulous documentation of every financial transaction within a business. These transactions span a spectrum of categories, including revenue, expenses, assets, liabilities, and equity. Accurate categorization forms the bedrock of accounting, an essential prerequisite.

Reporting with Key Financial Statements: The second component entails the creation of indispensable financial statements. These statements offer critical insights into a business's financial health. Three primary financial statements play a pivotal role: the Income Statement, the Balance Sheet, and the Cash Flow Statement. The Income Statement delineates revenue, expenses, and profit over a defined period. The Balance Sheet provides a snapshot of assets, liabilities, and equity at a specific point in time. The Cash Flow Statement tracks the flow of cash in and out of the business, a vital gauge of liquidity.

Analyzing the Data: The third and culminating phase is the analytical dimension. Here, raw numerical data transforms into actionable insights. Key metrics and ratios come to the forefront, offering a profound understanding of a business's financial dynamics. This analytical prowess empowers informed decision-making, highlights trends, identifies areas of improvement, and fuels strategic planning.

It is crucial to acknowledge that accounting is not an isolated, one-time activity performed solely in preparation for tax obligations. Rather, it constitutes an ongoing system vital for tracking financial data, monitoring performance, unveiling valuable insights, and facilitating prudent decision-making. It provides the means to gaze both into the past and into the future, aiding in financial forecasting.

To illustrate this concept holistically, consider the scenario of a burgeoning landscaping enterprise named " ZenithGardens". Initially modest in scale, it experiences rapid growth owing to exceptional service quality. As expansion becomes a natural progression, the business owner contemplates financial intricacies.

Questions arise about affordability, investment limits, and the genuine cost implications of expansion. These queries underscore the significance of accounting in guiding such pivotal business decisions.

Step 1: Recording Financial Transactions

The inaugural stage of the accounting process is the meticulous recording of every financial transaction transpiring within your business. This integral process is commonly referred to as bookkeeping or data entry. It is imperative to understand that every instance of monetary inflow or outflow must be diligently documented. This imperative applies without exception, requiring the recording of each and every transaction.

These financial transactions can be categorized into five primary types, each serving a distinct purpose:

Revenue: As a fundamental category, revenue encapsulates the monetary influx arising from the sale of products and services. In the context of our illustration, for " ZenithGardens," it encompasses the income derived from services such as mowing, fertilization, and tree planting.

Expenses: Expenses encompass the financial outlays incurred in the daily operation of your business. These expenses may span a range, including personnel-related costs (payroll), promotional expenses (advertising), and overhead costs (rent).

Assets: Assets represent valuable holdings owned by your company. These encompass a diverse array, ranging from tangible assets such as equipment to intangible assets like your brand name. Furthermore, liquid assets, including cash, fall under this classification.

Liabilities: Liabilities denote financial obligations typically owed by your business. This category encompasses loans, debts, lines of credit, unpaid invoices, and tax liabilities.

Equity: Commonly known as owner's equity, this term denotes your ownership stake in the business. It signifies the portion of assets financed by the business owners themselves, distinguishing it from external creditors.

Step 2: Creating financial statements based on transaction data.

There are three key financial statements that provide different views into the finances of a business:

Income Statement: The income statement shows a summary of a company's revenues, expenses, and profits (or losses) over a specific period, typically a month, quarter, or year. It helps answer the question of how profitable the business is during that period. It acts as a scorecard for your business's financial performance. For example, for the ZenithGardens Company, it would show revenue, the cost of services, and the resulting profit.

Balance Sheet: The balance sheet provides a snapshot of a company's financial position at a specific point in time. It outlines the company's assets (what it owns), liabilities (what it owes), and equity. The balance sheet helps you understand the company's financial health at a particular moment. For ZenithGardens Company, it would list assets like trucks and lawn mowers, liabilities such as loans and unpaid bills, and equity, which includes owner contributions and retained profits.

Cash Flow Statement: The cash flow statement tracks the movement of cash in and out of a business in real-time. It categorizes cash flows into three main sections: operating activities (cash generated from day-to-day operations), investing activities (cash related to buying or selling assets), and financing activities (cash related to borrowing or repaying loans and equity contributions). The cash flow statement helps answer questions such as whether the company is collecting payments from customers promptly, how investments and debt impact cash reserves, and how cash is being utilized. It provides insights into a company's liquidity.

These three financial statements together provide a comprehensive view of a business's financial performance, position, and cash flow. Analyzing them over time allows business owners and stakeholders to make informed decisions and monitor the financial health and trends of the company.

Step 3: Analyzing Financial Data

In the third stage of the accounting process, we embark on the transformative journey of turning raw numerical data into actionable insights. This phase is where the true magic transpires, as we leverage these insights to fortify and enhance the profitability of our business.

To achieve this, we engage in the calculation of key metrics and ratios. These metrics are our compass, offering invaluable insights into the financial dynamics of our business. Here are a few examples:

Profit on the Income Statement: This metric reveals your pricing power and sheds light on the profitability of your business. It answers the pivotal question of how profitable your enterprise truly is. Think of it as a scorecard for your business, with the ultimate goal being sustained profitability.

Current Ratio on the Balance Sheet: This ratio is instrumental in assessing liquidity risk. It provides a snapshot of your business's ability to meet its short-term financial obligations. An understanding of liquidity is paramount to ensuring the stability of your operations.

Cash Flow Statement: This document is pivotal for forecasting growth potential. It diligently tracks the real-time movement of cash within your business. It answers critical questions such as the timeliness of customer payments, the impact of investments or debt on your cash reserves, and the judicious allocation of your available cash resources.

Let's illustrate this concept with a practical example involving Roger, the owner of a tofu business, who sought the expertise of his accountant, Jenny, to bolster his profit margins.

Upon scrutinizing his income statement, Roger discovered that his profit margin was merely 10 percent. Jenny concurred with this assessment, cautioning Roger about the imminent risk of financial instability if he failed to take corrective measures.

Upon closer examination of his expenses, Jenny unearthed the root cause of the issue. Roger was incurring substantial costs by sourcing premium ingredients from Whole Foods, resulting in spiraling expenses beyond control.

Jenny's sage advice to Roger was to shift to locally sourced produce, a change that promised to reduce costs by a substantial 30 percent. This simple adjustment worked wonders. With the introduction of more affordable yet equally fresh produce, Roger not only boosted his profit margins but also reduced his prices, making his offerings more accessible to his customers.

The outcome was remarkable: Customers flocked back to Roger's restaurant, attracted by the newfound affordability without compromising on quality. Within a mere month, Roger's profit margin surged to an impressive 20 percent.

In conclusion, as we delve into this phase, you will undoubtedly encounter various facets: patterns, challenges, but most importantly, the potential for growth and success. However, it is crucial to underscore the importance of initiating rigorous financial tracking without delay. The adage "garbage in, garbage out" aptly illustrates that the quality of your financial data directly impacts the quality of decisions you can make. Hence, the imperative is to maintain clean, clear, and concise financial records, which serve as the bedrock for informed decision-making.

To recap our journey through this extensive topic, we have gained a comprehensive understanding of accounting's paramount role in the management and oversight of every facet of your business. We have emphasized that accounting is not merely a static system but an ongoing process encompassing the recording, reporting, and analysis of financial data. Furthermore, we have highlighted the three core principles of accounting: transactions, financial statements, and analysis, which collectively enable us to navigate the financial landscape of our businesses effectively.

As we conclude this chapter on accounting, we warmly invite you, our dear reader, to seriously consider QuickBooks Online for your small business accounting needs. Having delved into the fundamentals of accounting, you'll find QuickBooks Online an invaluable tool for seamlessly managing your financial records. Furthermore, we are excited to recommend an additional resource that will greatly enhance your understanding and efficiency in using this software: "QuickBooks Online for Beginners Bible Edition [2 Books in 1]," available on Amazon. Authored by the major experts on the subject, this comprehensive guide is the epitome of expertise and clarity. It meticulously walks you through every feature of

QuickBooks Online, from initial enrollment to mastering core operations. The book is enriched with detailed instructions and visual aids, providing an immersive learning experience. Each function within the software is thoroughly explained by experts, ensuring you can leverage QuickBooks Online to its fullest potential. This guide is more than just a manual; it's a journey that transforms you from a novice to a proficient user of QuickBooks Online, guided by the foremost authorities in the field.

Conclusion

As we arrive at the conclusion of this journey, you've acquired the fundamental knowledge necessary for your entrepreneurial path. It's essential to retain the valuable insights you've gained from these pages, but our invitation extends beyond that: continue to expand your knowledge and delve deeper into the intricacies of entrepreneurship as you prepare to build the future of your business.

Remember, success in entrepreneurship is a continuous process of learning, growth, and adaptation. The road ahead may be filled with challenges and uncertainties, but with determination and the wisdom you've gathered here, you're well-equipped to navigate the entrepreneurial landscape.

We extend our heartfelt wishes for your success and fulfillment. The journey you're about to embark upon is a testament to your vision, dedication, and courage.

Keep pushing on!

Best of luck for your extraordinary adventure!

By purchasing this book, you gain access to exclusive bonus content:

"The Small Business Masterclass"

This eBook delves deeper into the mindset of individuals embarking on an entrepreneurial journey from the ground up.

Access your copy of **"The Small Business Masterclass"** here:

Click on "Get your free eBook "Small Business Masterclass"" below the fields to leave your email, don't forget to sign up!

If you encounter any kind of problem with the QR code or the download of the free eBook, please let us know at the email address:

info@financeknightspublications.com

We will immediately take care of it.

We hope you enjoyed the book and found it useful.

We would be really grateful if you could leave us an **honest review** on Amazon. You would really help us out a lot!

In the meantime, we renew our greetings to you, your best allies

Finance Knights Publications

47867827R00071